Ammo Grrrll Hits The Target

Volume 1   2014

Dedication:

To My Dear Mr. Ammo Grrrll, Joe, for short. I know it is not easy being married to a Real Emotional Grrrll. You must alternate between peeling me off the ceiling and fork-lifting me out of the Slough of Despond and it can be exhausting.

You have oft bemoaned the fact that you are frequently "one emotion behind."

Sorry. And thanks for trying to keep up.

Thank God I can cook.

And To Those Without Whom This Book Would Not Exist:

With profound thanks to the Power Line Boys - Paul, John, George and Ringo.

No, wait, those are different guys, whom I also love. Paul Mirengoff, John Hinderaker, Steve Hayward, and my intrepid editor, Scott Johnson. Your site is awesome.

Thanks for letting me play in your reindeer games.

A DAY IN THE LIFE OF A FRIDAY COLUMNIST

Friday is my favorite day. And not just because it begins the weekend. TGIF and all that. Heck, when you're retired, it's all just six Saturdays and a Sunday anyway. No, it goes beyond that for me.

In my former profession, standup comedy, you never had to wait for a performance review of your work. The feedback was immediate. That was one of the things I loved about it, even on those unpleasant, but rare, occasions when it went badly.

Being an online Friday columnist with Commenters is similarly satisfying. I send my column to my editor, Scott, on Wednesday morning. If a political crisis or hot-button issue occurs, you can count on its being on a Thursday after I have already weighed in on the last crisis, or even, submitted an amusing little happy trifle, which was kind of my original mission. In this lightning-fast 24/7 news world, by the time the FOLLOWING Friday rolls around, I may as well be delivering a devastatingly-amusing analysis of the Lincoln-Douglas debates.

But on Fridays, my column is posted at 7 a.m. Minnesota time, and usually by the time I stagger to the coffee maker in Arizona at 6:00 a.m., there are a few dozen comments already. I don't get a lot else done on Fridays, I confess. People are so nice, so supportive, so witty, it makes me as happy as kind-hearted fans say the column makes them.

So, I originally thought to list as many "favorite" commenters as I could possibly remember:

You know the regulars: Heather, Deb, Tracy, Janna, David, Mary Louise, Bonnie, James, Abby, several Jims, Dorothy, Colleen, Alasdair, Daniel, Arnold, Kevin, Arlie Ray, Luis, two Michaels…

And then, especially without access to the old Facebook comments, I realized what would happen. I would forget somebody, probably several people -- as President Trump would say, "terrific people" -- and hurt their feelings.

I don't want any treasured regular commenter saying, "Well, what am I? Chopped liver?"

So, I'm just going to say to each and every Commenter THANK YOU. I THINK OF YOU ALL AS MY LITTLE FRIDAY FAMILY, and wish all manner of health, wealth and happiness to come your way.

However, having said that, one Commenter has, to my certain knowledge, never missed a week in nearly five years.

I must single out **Gary Davis**, retired Law Enforcement Officer from Alabama, for very special mention. His steadfast support has cheered, encouraged, and amused me, not that he should feel the slightest bit of pressure to continue, going forward. Roll Tide, Roll!

(I anticipate doing at least 3 or 4 more compilations in the future. Let's see just how amusing, flattering, or obsequious you each can be to see who gets the next Honorable Mention Slot. May I direct you to the Thesaurus for synonyms for "comic genius". Perhaps study things said in the *New York Times* or on CNN about President Obama. Light-Bringer works for me, although Donut-Bringer would be more accurate. I'm going to my laundry room right now to work on the crease in my pants.)

HOW I BECAME AMMO GRRRLL

In 2010, we moved to gun-friendly Red State Arizona from Minnesota, a state so Blue, it was the only state in the Union that didn't go for President Reagan either time.

My father had been an avid hunter – ducks, pheasants, and especially deer. Daddy was an excellent marksman and almost always came home with a deer strapped to his vehicle, causing my little sister – a future vegetarian -- to run and hide in the basement. Mama never hunted deer, but she hunted pheasant in her native South Dakota and was also a darn good shot.

But we had no handguns in our home. Heck, we didn't even lock our front door at night. Once in a great while there would be a story on television about a prison break in California. This would cause me to beg my parents to lock the door, "just in case" the miscreants formulated a cunning plan to hide out over 2,500 miles away.

It goes without saying that a small town in frigid Northern Minnesota where everyone knows everyone else, and their business, would be the perfect place for California convicts to blend in. I was an excitable and high-strung child who morphed seamlessly into a semi-neurotic but cheerful adult.

When several of our new friends in Arizona were enthusiastic gun collectors and target shooters, my husband, hereinafter Mr. AG, bought his first gun and looked online for an instructor. He found a great guy named Glenn, whom we dubbed Glenn the Gun Guy, or 3G for short.

Now at this exact moment in time, kids, Obama was President over all the land. And it came to pass that a great Ammo Drought occurred in which ammo became very scarce and strictly rationed. Since Mr. AG worked full-time, it became my part-time job to locate sources of – and stand in line for -- .40 caliber rounds for his Springfield XDM Semi-Automatic pistol.

It became a challenge, a game, and a sacred quest for me. I had never cottoned much to the notion that something was forbidden to me – because I was a girl or because I wasn't good enough and the like – and I developed a regular circuit from Dick's Sporting Goods to Walmarts all over the Metro area, to various sleazier emporia.

Soon, a hard-core of "regulars" we dubbed "the friendlies" got to know each other and pass on information. Sometimes, we would stand in line together for 3 or 4 hours at a time to snag the one box per customer allowed. It got to the point that if other desperate shooters didn't see me first or second in line, they knew no ammo was forthcoming.

At the same time, Mr. AG went back to Minnesota (and our other home) for the summer to tie up ends there and pursue some artistic interests. Alone in the house with a loaded weapon, I decided I should know what to do with it. Glenn became my instructor as well and, to everyone's great shock, not least of which was my own, I inherited my father's innate marksmanship coupled with my mother's discipline and persistence. Plus, Glenn is the best teacher I have ever had of any subject or skill.

I have never competed at shooting and probably never will. I don't have any desire to add a layer of stress to something that is so purely pleasurable to me. Similarly, even though I enjoy hot dogs (all beef/kosher), I will never try to beat that perennial skinny little Asian guy in a hot dog eating contest.

I am a pretty good shot. There are undoubtedly thousands, or tens of thousands of better shooters. But I do pretty well for a woman of late, late middle age who had never held a gun until age 67. And I just love the heck out of it!

My first task was to learn not to jump six inches every time someone in another lane at the Tactical Range fired a weapon. The second task was to wear appropriate clothing to avoid being hit in sensitive areas by hot flying brass.

Like all shooters, I quickly learned that one gun was not going to be enough. Before I injured my rotator cuff, it was not unusual for me to shoot three or four guns for two or three hours and go through hundreds and hundreds of rounds.

(I had originally thought that the major expense of target shooting would be the weapons. I was wrong. As everyone learns, it's the ammo – now needed in multiple calibers -- that makes it a relatively expensive hobby.)

But it still is cheaper than golf.

HOW IS THIS BOOK ORGANIZED?

In trying to figure out how to organize this compilation, several methods presented themselves. First, of course, I could just run the columns in the chronological order they ran on Power Line.

But that didn't seem all that interesting or fun. I decided to group them according to broad generalized categories with little pieces of new copy in between. The individual columns will still bear the dates on which they appeared in Power Line.

And to give the whole shebang a touch of class that the column does not usually possess, I decided to call the space between the categories Intermezzo.

I know what you're thinking, "AG, that SOUNDS pretty fancy, and Italian or French or something, but what the heck does it mean?"

Ask, and it shall be given unto you:

Definition of Intermezzo: *a short connecting instrumental movement in an opera or other musical work.*

Well, okay, I'm not all that sophisticated, but Mr. AG is. And also musical. It was his idea.

You know how typically an author will thank a bunch of people and then say that any errors are his and his alone? Not me. If you don't like the Intermezzo idea or the margins or the type face, it's all Mr. AG's fault. But, without his technical expertise, I would have had to just type and print every reader his or her personal copy. Yours might have been scheduled to arrive in June of 2028. So, there's that.

INTERMEZZO: THE ERMAS

When I first approached Scott Johnson to ask if he would be interested in a little humor column that would, initially at least, focus on "Thoughts" gleaned from standing in the ammo line at Walmart, he leapt on it. I sent him a sample column, expecting to hear back from him in a few days, and it appeared in the site in about three minutes. Yikes!

Scott had discussed often and self-deprecatingly, his Anger Management Problem. There is a great deal in the current culture and political situation to make a person's head explode. He hoped that I would mostly write light and breezy HUMOROUS offerings, partly as therapy for him personally.

As the months of columns went by, I also found myself being drawn into the Swirling Vortex of Rage. While I hope most of the columns still displayed some sort of "wit", there were those ventings and screeds that were decidedly less funny. And here we get into the Lincolnesque observation that "you can't please all the people all of the time." Well, he said "fool" all the people, but you take my meaning.

And, camps developed that mostly liked one or the other. A recurring "character" in my columns – The Paranoid Texan -- who, I assure you, is a real-life guy, and a great one at that, prefers the light and breezy, more generic, less political offerings. He's not much of a political guy. He likes good dogs and Irish Whiskey, the San Antonio Spurs and firearms.

Another friend – Mike – is okay with the lighter stuff, which he has dubbed somewhat disparagingly, "The Erma Bombeck Collection", but he vastly prefers the Red Meat diatribes, potshots and tirades. We first connected after a particularly personal response to Hillary's calling me and all my friends Deplorables.

Now, I am pleased as punch when anyone compares me to the late, great Arizonan, Ms. Bombeck. She was a brilliant writer. A religious Catholic and family person, she was kind of a Trojan Horse who managed to sneak some very important and serious stuff into her seemingly-light offerings. She was one of my earliest heroines and influences as a teenage writer.

So, I thought I would begin this compilation of columns with what Mike calls The Ermas. We can start out relaxed and copacetic and work our way up to Mildly Annoyed and then, Seriously Upset.

Whichever you prefer, enjoy.

But before we get to the Ermas –

TA-DA! – the Column that Began It All.

March 30, 2014

My Power Line editor, Scott Johnson wrote the following: Our old friend Susan Vass has had a productive career in stand-up comedy making people laugh for a living. I'm not sure if she's still working, but she still thinks funny thoughts. She has forwarded current meditations under the pseudonym Ammo Grrrll in columns she calls "Thoughts from the Ammo Line."

Ammo Grrrll writes:

A few years ago, I moved from a blue to a red planet. No, wait, I moved from Minnesota to Arizona, but my point still stands. A metric ton of tedious lip service is paid to the concept of "diversity" in Minnesota (motto: "It's Not Just the Landscape that Is Lily White!")

My dusty little village in Arizona is the most diverse place I have ever lived. There's obviously so much intermarriage that people no longer fit neatly into Census Bureau boxes. But, you've got your Native-Americans; you've got your African-Americans; you've got your Latinos, many of them legal; and you've got your Geezer-Americans, retirees of every hue and creed, dumping their Social Security checks into the slot machines and supporting the Native-Americans in a beautiful Circle of Life.

Everybody gets along. Everybody eats at the same three local diners. Everybody is polite. Everybody is smiley and friendly, even teenagers! Why?

Because everybody is armed to the teeth – cowboys, geezers, Iraqi vets, tattooed Latinos, nuns.

You see ranchers ambling through Walmart with .45 caliber 1911s on their hips in glorious Open Carry and nobody even bats an eyelash. In Minnesota, someone would dive under the Size 4XL Clearance Rack and call SWAT. In Arizona, you say "Good morning," and the cowboy tips his Stetson and says, "Ma'am."

A cousin visiting from Los Angeles who travels almost exclusively in metrosexual circles, looked in wide-eyed wonder at the much-maligned denizens of Walmart and exclaimed: "Oh my God! ACTUAL MEN!!"

I am at the Walmart ammo case every morning hoping to find .22LR, .40s or 9 millimeter bullets for our guns. I target-shoot about 350 rounds twice a week, so it's a part-time job to keep up. The new ammo – if there is any – is put into the case after 7:00 a.m. The line sometimes forms as early as 4:00 a.m. I'm almost always first in line except on Saturdays. American Rifleman magazine says there are now five million women shooters, up over 46 percent since 2001, which partially explains the ammo shortage. You go, grrrlls!

Contrary to anti-gun propagandists who assert that the only gun owners are certifiably insane old white men, the ammo line also reflects our diversity. The guy who beats me there on Saturdays is a black great-grandpa I'll call Steve, on account of that's his name. He shows up pre-dawn after his swing-shift job. Today he is wearing a T-shirt that says "Ammo is scarce – there will be no warning shots." He brings a Mexican co-worker with him this Saturday. Tim, my young white personal banker, stops by in a suit to say hi, but he is shopping for fishing gear, not bullets. He doesn't need bullets.

Oh, not because he doesn't shoot. Everybody shoots. He is a "reloader" – he makes his own ammo. Problem solved.

THE DUSTY LITTLE VILLAGE

May 23, 2014

When we first moved to our Dusty Little Village (DLV) in Arizona, occasionally people from one or another Big City would come to visit. They would notice that to get to our new home from the airport, they would have to travel roughly 20 miles southeast from suburban Phoenix through lots and lots of empty desert.

"Why in God's name do you live out here in the middle of nowhere?" they would ask. "There's NOTHING between Chandler and your house!"

Well, that depends on your definition of "nothing."

Today on the way back from shlepping my husband's gun to the gunsmith, and running through a couple hundred rounds at the range, I saw our stunning herd of wild horses that number close to 100 now, with many new babies which knowledgeable cowgirls call "foals." They were no more than 20 feet from the road and many drivers were snapping photos with their cellphones, a few even pulling over to do so, if they were also smoking or eating. The wild horses generally pasture just past the Cement Factory. Hey, city slickers, do YOU have a Cement Factory? I thought not.

I also saw a number of fascinating dust devils – violent, isolated little dust-tornadoes – that look as exotic as Moses' burning bush.

Many cacti were in bloom with spectacular flowers in fuscia and Day-Glo Yellow. And the dignified old Saguarros – the State symbol of Arizona – cover the landscape like sentries alert for unwelcome intrusions such as over-priced coffee emporia or California taxpayers who voted to ruin California fleeing to Arizona and then saying, "Hey, let's run that experiment again."

I had the opportunity to buy "fresh seafood" from a truck by the side of the road. Highly-perishable "Sea"-food, hundreds of miles from the nearest sea, sold by an unlicensed, undocumented gentleman from a pickup in 103-degree weather. What could possibly go wrong?

Could there be anything worse to buy from a roadside truck? Well, yes there could.

Just a couple more miles down the road, yet another pickup had deeply-discounted mattresses on offer. Who could even guess at the provenance of roadside mattresses? "What's this? Bloodstains?" "No, is camo." "Ah. Well, no harm, then." Nothing clears guests out faster than letting it slip that the $12.95 mattress in the guest casita came from a roadside pickup. Unless it's the gamy shrimp in their mini-fridge.

You call it nuthin'. I call it home.

WEIGHT LOSS

May 30, 2014

I read with great interest both my Power Line editor, Scott's, recent post on his weight-loss paradigm, and the many sincere and helpful comments readers shared. For those success stories, mazel tov, and may you all go from strength to strength!

Not to pull rank or anything, but I consider myself to be An Expert on weight loss. Oh, sure, I haven't been a van driver — which would qualify me to stare like a deer in headlights into the camera and lie inarticulately on national security — but in the arena of weight loss, dudes, my credentials are nearly without peer.

I have lost well over 400 lbs. It's the truth, my hand to God!

Unfortunately, it is the same 20 lbs., lost and regained some 20 times.

And here is my best advice: GIVE UP. At 5'3" in heels, I have a better chance of being called for goal-tending in the NBA than I do of maintaining my goal-weight for over 3 days.

Let me break it down for you: if you give up smoking, or even heroin, it's a binary decision. As long as you continue to say "No," you are succeeding. I smoked 3 packs a day in college, quit cold turkey, and have never had another cigarette. I do sometimes hang around outdoor places where addicted employee-pariahs are forced to congregate, so that I can get a second-hand contact high. I plan to start smoking unfiltered Luckies (do they still exist?) when I'm 90. The tobacco, they claimed, was "toasted"! Yum! But I digress…

Eating is NOT a binary decision. Every single day, you must make wise decisions, 3 or 4 or 5 times a day, depending on your paradigm with allotted meals and snacks. What ARE the chances, seriously, that you are never going to make an unwise decision? That after weeks of gluten-free or low carb crap, you aren't going to go from gluten to glutton and order a Deep Dish Pizza, a side of Fettucini Alfredo and a whole Carrot Cake for dessert?

But the worse news is that it doesn't even take a major freak-out. If you take in just 100 calories a day more than your body uses for fuel (one small chocolate chip cookie, say), that's about 10 pounds you will put on in a year. My husband burns calories like the Obamas burn money on vacation. I, on the other hand, have a metabolism so efficient that, if I were a car, I could go from coast to coast on a couple gallons of gas. Call me Volt.

Hold it! Did I say, "Give up"? Ammo Grrrll has a milestone high school reunion coming up in 3 months, so it's time to lose those last few pounds, assuming that "few" is defined as 15-20. I found a "Thyroid Detox" diet in the most recent issue of "Woman's World" – a fabulously optimistic magazine I buy weekly that has headlines like "Lose 45 Pounds By Friday on the Chocolate Diet!"

The Thyroid Detox entails eating 10 servings of fruits and vegetables a day. I bought a whole bunch of wretched vegetables at Walmart and I put them in that little bin at the bottom of the fridge that I call The Rotter. Not to brag, but after 5 days, I have already lost .2 of a pound! Wish me luck. And stay tuned.

ACCIDENTS

June 6, 2014

Last week my shooting instructor fell in a practice run for his motorcycle precision drill team and injured his foot. A biker enthusiast in an unfortunate mishap.

One of our regular Wednesday night poker players (5 years in Iraq), sustained a broken neck from an IED and spent 19 months in hospital. A hero.

And Ammo Grrrll? This morning I woke up with shooting pains in my upper back and right bicep. From a repetitive stress injury from playing Candy Crush for five straight hours. An idiot with OCD.

This is not my first rodeo with repetitive stress injuries. Several years ago, I began doing cross-stitch and embroidery on complicated baby quilts with thousands of stitches, and did it compulsively until I could barely lift my right arm above my shoulder. You perform ANY small motion enough times, be prepared to suffer the consequences.

I also sustained a "Sudoku Injury" in the form of a back spasm from leaning over at an odd angle at the dining room table working on a 6-star puzzle in a "Mensa Level" puzzle book. Yes, I can hear you wondering what a person with such a long learning curve is doing with anything with the label "Mensa" on it. Point taken.

Some people hurt their backs lifting automobiles off accident victims, or doing the firefighter's carry with a dead-weight unconscious person in a burning building. Or EMTs carrying an overweight heart attack victim down 3 flights of stairs on a gurney. But it takes a special person to hurt herself on a pointless 9-box Japanese puzzle.

So, if you ever see me hobbling, limping, or with an arm in a sling, please do me the favor of not asking, "How did this happen?"

If you've ever played peek-a-boo with a baby, you know that he will NEVER tire of it. You can do it until the cows come home, and it will always be exactly as fresh and funny to him as the first time. Most of us grow out of this stage and develop the ability to be bored. In fact, eventually, you will become either a teenager or a rich, decadent piece of Eurotrash in a Fellini film, and then you will be bored by EVERYTHING.

One of the things I like about myself is that I take immense pleasure from dozens of small things, a trait I learned from my dear mother. She is 93 and, in our daily phone call, will say things like "Daddy and I went to McDonald's and split a coffee and cherry pie, and it was just so much fun!"

So, I have almost no capacity for boredom. I can enjoy the same music, same food, same movies and books over and over. And also over. It's just that – like that baby – I don't always know when to stop. But, I'll stop writing now. I have to finish my quilt by early afternoon so I can start another one as soon as I get past Level 1286 in Candy Crush.

HOW HOT IS IT?

June 20, 2014

Many winter residents of Arizona are escapees from colder climes such as Canada, Michigan and Minnesota. Wonderful people in the main, they bring their money, amusing accents, and frugal tipping habits to our Dusty Little Village (DLV) and then they go home in late March or April, mercifully, before they can vote.

They swim in the community pool any day that is over 45 degrees and wear shorts and ill-advised tank tops all winter long. Is there any garment less attractive than the tank top, which mostly features armpits? Meanwhile native Arizonans are bundled up in scarves and down coats if the temperatures dip below a frigid 60°.

As a former Minnesotan, I am accustomed to having an Emergency Kit in my trunk, consisting of jumper cables, a shovel, a bag of sand or kitty litter, hand warmers, matches, flares, blankets, scarves, mittens, sleeping bags, and several granola bars that have to be unappealing enough not to be eaten in advance of an emergency. The recommended candy bars don't stand a chance of even making it to the car, let alone an emergency.

So, my first complete summer in my DLV came as quite the shock. Our hottest day was 119°, a truly ridiculous temperature which elicits a constant strong desire to shut Heaven's oven door. My neighbor, a charming native Texan who, not to be judgmental, may also be crazy, trimmed his tree for several hours on that day. I sat entombed in my house with all the shutters and blinds closed and the AC set to 80° – still 40 degrees cooler than outdoors! For those keeping score at home, 119° is nearly 21 degrees higher than body temperature. And your body cares.

Although 119° was our record last summer, we also had over 100 days in a row over 100°. The heat is brutal and absolutely relentless, almost a physical presence, like the cold in January up North. And fuggettabout it being a "dry" heat. It is often surprisingly humid. Whiskey, Tango, Foxtrot??!!

You learn to put a little white towel in your car to cover your steering wheel. You buy one of those windshield covers, but I hardly ever use mine because of the difficulty of trying to fold it up again, like the damn roadmaps of yore. You are willing to park up to three blocks away in order to park in "the shade," which is defined as any sliver of darkness by a twig. You shop for groceries at 5:00 a.m. at Bashas', the only grocery store with an extended sun-cover over their parking lots, God bless 'em. I even have a little garden glove in my fanny-pack with which to touch metal, like my car door handle. I'm serious as a heart attack.

And now my Emergency Kit consists of several gallons of water, sunscreen, a white shirt and long white cotton pants, an umbrella, a kiddie pool, a wide-brimmed hat, and more water.

I love Arizona anyway. Did I ever mention the six scorpions I have killed in my house? We'll save that for another day.

MARRIAGE

July 11, 2014

Awhile back two sweet Commenters kiddingly asked about Ammo Grrrll's marital status while making kind remarks about my work.

My neighbor, the slightly-paranoid Texan, was against my writing columns in the first place because he thought it might attract "weirdos." But my logical husband (Mr. Ammo Grrrll, who is much more macho than that sounds...) reminded him that your prudent stalker would tend to avoid a lady with a nickname that mentioned bullets, despite the attractive picture that Scott dug up on the Internet. A picture, by the way, that is every bit as current as the picture of Queen Elizabeth on Canadian money. Which I believe is her high school graduation picture where she was elected Homecoming Queen for practice.

So, yes, Ammo Grrrll is married. And has been married for a very very extremely very long time. We're already on our third bottle of Tabasco Sauce. Seriously, in 3 years we will celebrate our Golden Anniversary, Lord willing and the Creek don't rise.

"How did you stay happily married for almost half a century," you ask? "And, while we're at it, isn't 'happily married' an oxymoron like Over-eaters Anonymous?" Hang on, and I will give you some valuable marital advice which I feel qualified to dispense having been married since I was a teenager.

They tell trial lawyers never to ask a witness a question they don't already know the answer to. It's similar in marriage – never ask a question you don't WANT to know the answer to. For example, I have never once asked "Do these pants make my butt look big?" Or, "Who among my friends do you think is most attractive?" Nothing good can come of this.

Avoid hypothetical discussions like the plague. There is no point in fighting about what you would do with the money if you won the Lottery. First of all, your chances of winning the Lottery are identical whether you buy a ticket or not. Secondly, every article I've ever read about Lottery winners says the money ruined their lives; and thirdly, why waste a night sleeping on the couch because you would refuse to pay off my siblings' mortgages and don't want to buy a houseboat just because you get seasick? Hypothetically.

Outside of a structured therapy environment, trying to have a "You tell me one thing that bugs you about me and I'll tell you one thing that bugs me about you" discussion is far less productive than one might imagine. It never ends with "one" and somehow the offenses never seem equivalent, such as, "It bugs me when you leave the toilet seat up," versus, "It bugged me when you gave that Nigerian guy your cellphone number and our bank account number so he could get those gold bars out of Nigeria. Also, your family is insane."

Ha ha. That last one was a little joke. And that is the real advice: love, forgiveness, respect, patience, and most critically, a sense of humor. Oh, and also a compatible spice tolerance level is helpful. Ammo Grrrll likes Curried Szechuan Jalapenos, and Mr. Ammo Grrrll cannot handle Mint Dental Floss. But somehow we make it work.

NAME TAGS: A SPORTING CHANCE!

July 25, 2014

If you live long enough, eventually you will have difficulty remembering the names of anyone you haven't known since grade school or aren't currently married to. This usually begins about the time you get your first mailing from AARP (the Addled Attempting to Recognize People).

Babe Ruth just called everybody "Kid," which is one approach. I often call people "Hon," and, if you should land a PR job with the Obama Administration, you could call news anchors "Dude."

Another approach is to just up and move to a new state, hypothetically, Arizona, and try hard not to meet any new people.

What you should NOT do is attempt to fake it. For one thing, people are stubbornly resistant to throwing you a life preserver. How many times have you been talking to someone you kinda sorta recognize but whose name you do not know and your wife or co-worker comes up to stand beside you, expecting an introduction? If she is a GOOD wife who knows you can only remember the names of ancient baseball players or obscure cowboy action actors from your childhood, she will put out her hand and say, "I'm Ammo Grrrll, nice to meet you." And do you think the doofus will say his or her name back? Oh no, that would be too helpful.

Continuing the theme of faking it: It will also not behoove you to try to fish around for some clue. Sample scenario at a party:

Vaguely Familiar Person Who Seems to Know YOU: "Hey, Arnie,

great to see you!"
You (Arnie): "Wow, yeah, how you been?"
VFP: "Fine."
You (madly searching for clues): "How's work?"
VFP: "Oh you know, same old, same old."
You: "The family good?"
VFP: "You bet."
You: "Well, I've got to get to the Post Office before the price of stamps changes. Whoa! Look at that hottie over there!"
VFP: "That's my wife."
You: "Sure, I knew that."

It has long been my contention that it's not what you don't know in Life that hurts you the most, but what you know for sure that isn't true. If you are doing a crossword puzzle and the clue is "an intrusive govt agency" in 4 letters, and you're sure it's OSHA, when it's NLRB, you are going to be heading down the wrong path at full speed.

This happened to my mother several years ago. She was in her hometown mall with her adult grandson, Marc, a very proper, easily-embarrassed young man, when she ran into a woman she hadn't seen for some time, who she was absolutely certain was a lady named Betty. The following conversation took place that has become legend in our family:

Lady: "Well, goodness gracious, you're looking wonderful, Dorothy!"
Mom: "How sweet of you to say that! How's your husband?"
Lady: (long pause) "He died three years ago. You were at the funeral."
Mom: "Oh my goodness, I'm so sorry. I thought you were Betty B."
Lady: "No, I'm Shirley S."
Mom: (waiting for floor to open up) "Well, for Pete's sake. I could

have sworn..."
Marc: (sprinting away, blending into crowd. Grandma? What Grandma? I've never seen this woman in my life.)

I realize that in Minnesota you can't even convince the electorate that an ID should be required to vote. One man, one vote is so yesterday. New motto: one felon, one illegal, 300 votes for Franken! But, I think with our aging Boomers, it would be very helpful to have mandatory nametags. Give us a sporting chance to avoid humiliation.

LET'S MOVE!

August 1, 2014

Though regular readers of this column will not be surprised to hear that Ammo Grrrll is not a general fan of either Obama, I do have some sympathy for the First Lady's campaign to reduce the size of America's Weeble Children. The "Let's Move 60!" campaign to get the inert little lard-butts to play hard for an hour a day would be as incomprehensible to someone in the 50s as a pitch to get men to just *TRY* sex. "*C'mmmmon*, just once, it's *FUN!*"

In the '50s whenever we weren't in school, our mothers threw us out of the house at first light and unlocked the doors when our daddies came home for supper. Oh, if we were lucky, we might have a peanut butter sandwich on Wonder Bread handed to us through the doggie door, but, in general, we were on our own for vast hours a day. If we had a little pocket change, we might split a Popsicle or purchase several penny packages of dyed sugar called "Lik-M-Aid" that you licked out of your grubby little unsanitized hand.

And all we did was run around like lunatics and play death-defying games that are now illegal. Like Mumblety-peg which involved a working jack-knife, or Dodge Ball, Red Rover, Keep Away or an uplifting game called Kill The Man With the Ball, which was everything the name implies. Now the little Special Snowflakes need a helmet to play Candyland.

We played whatever game was in season – baseball, basketball, football – either until it was too dark to see the ball, or until our mothers called us for the third time, using our MIDDLE NAMES, or until the first time our fathers whistled. Oops, crap, that's

DADDY – gotta run! Daddies were in charge and everybody had one. Everybody. Some were nice, most were scary, veterans home from the War, and all adult males were Misters (or Sirs below the Mason-Dixon Line.)

Even the girly-girls who were less tomboyish than Ammo Grrrll, jumped rope for hours, roller-skated, ice-skated, (sometimes on the same early June day in Minnesota), and rode bicycles. And that was the town kids, of course. The country kids had chores up the wazoo. Homegrown crews of little farm laborers only with fewer rights than migrants. Where was Cesar Chavez when my friend Loretta had to pick rocks out of fields or weed the strawberries all weekend?

And not ONE kid was fat, not one! Tubby, in the Little Lulu comics was more or less mythological. Now our kids sit and play electronic games or watch television or fiddle with their phones and computers. Eating giant plates of fast food instead of nourishing Lik-M-Aid. No wonder they are fat. They don't burn 50 calories in a day.

To me there are few sights more pathetic than an entire family ignoring each other in a restaurant, each person tapping away on his or her own phone. Brothers should be punching each other and informing the father who started it; and the mother should be carping about how much cheaper she could have made the chicken at home and the younger sister should be repeating everything her big sister says until the big sister bawls in frustration. You know, RELATING! Good clean family fun!

STUCK ON STUPID

August 8, 2014

At the risk of appearing to pander, I am going to assert that, based on the quality of comments, Power Line regulars are smarter than the average bears. However, I have read that in surveys, almost everyone rates himself or herself as "above average" in intelligence. Clearly, if "average" has any meaning at all, this cannot be true; demonstrably, in some cases.

As unseemly as it is to still be going on about it half a century later, Ammo Grrrll was, in fact, one of four valedictorians of her high school class with a perfect 4.0 average. Hard as it is to imagine from my accompanying wildly-outdated picture, Ammo Grrrll was not a cute cheerleader or a beautiful Prom Queen. No, seriously. This is all she had to hang her hat on. And so it is with a heavy heart that I will now show you how far the mighty have fallen.

Yesterday I made a delicious and healthy Smoothie in my blender. When it came time to wash the blender, naturally I unscrewed the base with the sharp blades and washed that separately and carefully. Then I washed the glass pitcher part and commenced to rinse it. A blender with no bottom becomes a perfect funnel. With the wide top part under a running faucet and the bottom part pointed at what we at the gun range call "center mass," the obvious will ensue. "And the 4th Runner Up in the Girls Gone Stupid Wet T-Shirt Contest is…"

This was neither the first time I had done this, nor the most boneheaded play of my day.

I purchased an Indoor-Outdoor thermometer system to get daily confirmation that Arizona is, indeed, hot. (But only from April through October, so no worries.) Rather than bother my husband, my yard guy, or my outrageously handy, kindly retired neighbor, I vowed to put on my Big Girl Pants and do it myself! A college graduate should be able to read simple directions and install 5 batteries in two units, even if she does have a uterus.

And so, I did everything the accompanying brochure told me to do in the exact order specified and proudly placed the remote sensor outdoors. And waited. Alas, the values on the indoor unit's screen never changed. I installed different batteries. No change.

I was hunting for the receipt to return the clearly defective unit to Walmart, when Enrique, the aforementioned yard guy came in for a Coke. Enrique is not a college graduate. Though he can fix, build, or do anything and probably could have been a brain surgeon, he had to quit school after 4th grade to help support his large, fatherless family in Mexico.

He glanced at the unit, tried with limited success to keep from laughing at Senora, and removed the clear plastic film with the fake values printed on it that the unit came with. It worked perfectly. Oh my. Well, except for the fact that it claimed to be 165 degrees, straining credulity even for Arizona. Enrique moved the unit from the direct sunlight, as the brochure had recommended, and it plunged to a seasonally pleasant and accurate 107.

I have been retired for several years now. But, should I have to return to work, my resume might read: "Un-recent Sociology Major seeks work. Excellent at standing in lines."

FRIENDSHIP

October 24, 2014

The New York Times—faithful, fawning Boswell to Obama's Johnson (it's a literary reference, grow up) – informed us recently that The President is "seething" over his minions' incompetence! A once-prestigious paper reduced to being a childish narcissist's mood ring. What if the rest of us mere mortals had such powerful friends as Pinch, Punch and Little Paunch who would print any drivel we fed them as news? This suggested the topic of Friendship and that is what we will discuss today.

I have pretty rigorous standards for what constitutes true friendship. I am blessed with perhaps a dozen really close friends evenly divided between men and women. Dozens more are valued acquaintances. And that's nice, too. Not everyone is destined to be a soulmate.

How do we know, often at an early age, who we are going to bond with for life? What is that alchemy? In romantic attachments, of course, you have sexual attraction which unsentimental scientists tell us is just pheromones. What is it in friendship? Commenters, please share your thoughts. I am fascinated by this mystery.

Of my closest friends, one I met when we were 6 and the twins of Road Trip fame when we were 14. In the latter case, had our last names not started with "B" so that we sat next to each other in class, it may never have happened. Think of that! Bonded for life because of the alphabet! At the end of the movie *Stand By Me* the narrator says: "I never had any friends later on like the ones I had when I was 12. Jesus, does anyone?"

I do, actually. In adulthood I became great friends with two neighbors, from the serendipity of having bought a house next door. One neighbor's motorcycle buddies also became beloved friends. Being retired is almost like being a kid again, only with more money. You can go ring the bell and ask if Randy or Angela can come out and play.

Like the colored terror threat levels, I have constructed a handy Friendship Level chart.

Level 1 (Beige) – You know these people very casually. They will come to a party that YOU throw and drink your beer and eat your chips. Some of them will never be invited back.

Level 2 (Puce) – These people will actually trouble themselves to host a party to which you are invited. You see them a couple times a year like New Year's Eve or Superbowl.

Level 3 (Periwinkle) – People who will hang out and engage in mutual activities. Men tend to share activities while women share heart-stuff and recipes. I once had a co-worker named Ted whose "best friend" Jim filed for divorce without Ted's ever knowing there was anything wrong with the marriage! This would be unthinkable for a pair of women friends.

Level 4 (Silver) – Now we're getting serious. These friends will help you move. Cultivate people who own pickups. Mr. Ammo Grrrll and I helped two sets of "Silver" friends with equally wretched Minnesota moves, one in July and one in January. In the first, it was 98 and humid; the second was 30 below zero with a stiff wind. Good times, good times.

Level 5 (Gold) – These folks know your very soul. They will pick you up at LAX at rush hour, knowing that you will do the same.

They will take a 3:00 a.m. call if you are depressed or anxious. They will commiserate with you when you are down, and will rejoice with you without jealousy when good things happen to you. If you are lucky, this level includes your spouse.

Some Gold friends will clean up an extremely-deceased rabbit on your patio. And shoot pigeons – winged rats, really – off your roof. Hypothetically, because that would violate HOA rules and a bunch of other picky laws.

(Memo to self: check on the Statute of Limitations for bb-gun infractions before sending to Scott. Even though nothing happened. Plenty of reasonable explanations for dead pigeon. Google "Incidents of Pigeon Suicide: More frequent than commonly thought?" See also: "Pigeon Gangs and Drive-Bys – The Craps vs. the Bloods").

One thing I do know for sure: friendship needs quality time and effort. Trite but true, to have a friend you have to be a friend. And sometimes that means picking up the phone, sitting down to email, reaching out to comfort, when you'd rather just watch Seinfeld re-runs or ESPN. Friends not only enrich your life; they lengthen it. Call one today.

ABBY

February 2, 2015

A few weeks ago, Mr. Ammo Grrrll and I had the pleasure of meeting some new friends from Florida who are fans of the Power Line boys and devoted readers of *Thoughts From the Ammo Line*. Abby and Ken were in Arizona for their delightful tradition of spending New Year's Eve in the Grand Canyon, a tradition dating back to 1996!

Abby, a self-described Florida cracker, was rather more taken with snow than your Minnesota-raised Ammo Grrrll who prefers vacations in which tan, attractive men bring you drinks with umbrellas. Adventurous Abby went out in the snow and made a Snow Angel and then bought a saucer-type sled. We are virtually the same age and if I were to rank activities I'd like to pursue at fifty-eight(een), "sledding" would come in at #537, right after "exercising with Harry Reid," "sharing a luge with Michael Moore," and "Cleaning up after any Million Man March."

She then found a smallish hill – OK, not the Swiss Alps, but a hill nevertheless – and went down it in her saucer three times. They left the saucer with relatives in Prescott in order to play with it again next year. Now, I know people who have gone sky-diving without Depends, who have bungee-jumped in the actual Swiss Alps, who have taken swooping helicopter rides over volcanoes. Having just seen American Sniper, we won't even mention combat veterans as that is a whole 'nother (as we say in Minnesota) category of courage.

So, it was not so much the feat itself that wowed me, but her overall spirit of adventure. She's just open to new things, new people, new experiences, and that's a wonderful and enviable way to be. I am always impressed when people take on adventurous projects. I am the Queen of Wussie-Pants Homebodies, one small ratchet up from an agoraphobic.

Even as a kid, I preferred the Merry-go-Round to the Roller Coaster. My friend Angela rides her own motorcycle, can fly a plane, drive a tractor, and looks for the highest, most terrifying Roller Coaster she can find, assembled by the drunk carnie with the fewest teeth. I need somebody to hold my hand on The Small, Small World ride, preferably someone with a Nerf bat to knock that hideous song out of my head afterwards.

Now, many women and not a few men are uncomfortable around firearms and I love them, so I guess that would qualify as mildly-adventurous. Jerry Seinfeld claims that the Number One fear in America is speaking in public; hence, 30 years of standup comedy would also place me outside most people's comfort zone, especially that of my high school classmate, Wayne, who called in sick every day when there was an Oral Book Report due, for as long as it took for the teacher to forget it. (In a croaking whisper:) "Sorry. This laryngitis seems to be hanging on a few weeks...and I also have a touch of leprosy...I may have to just hand in a written report..."

Were I to be coaxed out of retirement, say with vast amounts of cash, I think I would now combine the two, the hobby and the career. Standup with a firearm could markedly improve audience response. Remember all those Westerns where some psychotic guy would shoot at a poor victim's feet, laugh uproariously and say, "Dance, yellowbelly, dance!"? Imagine the surprising fun of someone shooting close to an audience member's head chortling, "Laugh, you humorless twit, laugh!" No? A girl can dream.

Mr. Ammo Grrrll, Juris Doctor, says "tough on Liability Insurance, tough on innocent audience members behind the reluctant laugher." Hey, I bet you shoot at just one and pretty soon the whole place is laughing like both lawyers when a judge cracks a joke. "Ha, ha, Your Honor, now that's funny!"

A story is told that a famous Chasidic rabbi informed his disciples that, at the age of 90, he was going to visit Switzerland. His flock was horrified. "But Master, you are too old for such a journey!" and he replied, "Well, this is the youngest age I have left. Soon I will meet my Maker and what will I tell Him when He asks, 'Yossi, what did you think of My Alps?'."

Abby appears to be fixin' to leave nothing undone. May she live long and prosper. Me, I'll have to tell the Almighty: "Well, I saw a lot of movies set in the Alps…Good job, there! Seriously! Have you heard the one where the horse goes into the bar and…"

So, dear readers and Commenters, what's still left on your bucket list? What's the most scary, adventurous thing you have ever done that's already checked off? Teaching your teenager to drive doesn't count. Neither does giving your wife an electric frying pan for an anniversary.

VALENTINE'S DAY

February 13, 2015

Well, fellas, Valentine's Day is tomorrow, so you still have a little time to get a box of candy, a dozen roses, or at least a card. Some ladies like the Victoria's Secret stuff, but others think of it as more of a gift FOR you rather than FROM you. But if it jerks her bobber, go for it! Who doesn't like the breezy feel of aerated undies?

Mr. Ammo Grrrll has no truck with the nonsense of what he calls "Hallmark--invented holidays," so I know I'm gettin' nuthin' again. But, to be fair, he does give me lovely, random gifts just when he feels like it, so it's all good. He just won't be shamed into it by Hallmark.

I'm pretty sure that Valentine's Day is not celebrated in school nowadays. Too much wrong with it; first of all, it's a holiday named after a saint which would be offensive to dozens of protected groups, including party-pooping atheists. Then, too, sending Valentines to your classmates would be fraught with gender peril. And lastly, there's the matter of heart-shaped sugar cookies with pink frosting that would send the First Lady and her henchpersons into a tizzy. Maybe a Carrot--Arugula--Lima Bean Cookie would pass muster. Yum.

But, back in the day, Valentine's Day was a much--anticipated event to the grade school crowd. Prep took a good week, although you would never tell your mother you had volunteered her to make six dozen frosted heart cookies until the night before.

You would make your Valentine's Box in Art Class out of a

shoebox covered in construction paper and doilies. A printed list of your classmates was sent home, with first name and, often, last initial to cover all the Kathys, Marys, Lindas, and Johns, Bobbys, and Jims. (These are now names that have mostly disappeared, but will be back as "old-fashioned" and cool in another 50 years. Last time I visited my old gradeschool, there were names on the lockers and not a single name was in existence when I was there. Taylor? Keneesha? Jose?)

Your exceptionally-thrifty mother would buy you a jumbo packet of the cheesiest, cheapest crap Valentine cards she could find. Even the glue on the envelopes was worthless and had to be supplemented with Scotch Tape. Whatever the writers were paid, it was too much. One card featured a puppy and the sentiment "Dog-gone it, be my Valentine." Oh, for clever!

The teachers in the 50s had not heard of "self--esteem," and if they had, would have been against it. But they guarded against hurt feelings by insisting that every kid had to send every other kid a Valentine. Nobody could be left out. So, you had to struggle to find the blandest card to send to that weird little boy who ate library paste. And, of course, the most "romantic" card would be sent to the curly--haired boy who made your little nine-year-old heart go pitter-pat. You would imagine him opening the card, seeing your signature, and realizing at last that you loved him. Perhaps – be still my heart! – he would send the same card back to you! Or at least stop shoving you off the monkey bars.

But, no. He sent you the "dog-gone" one. And the romantic one came from Library Paste Boy. Ewwwww! Well, at least, you reckoned, if we get married, dinner will be easy.

There was also a suck-up Valentine for the teacher. Normally, this was not a problem.

There is a myth that all teachers are selfless, child-loving mentors and role models. Like all stereotypes, there are enough fine examples who fit the profile to ring true. I could name half a dozen who were tough but fair, inspirational, and thoroughly professional.

However, there were also lazy, incompetent time-servers. Our Fourth Grade selection was particularly bleak as both classes were taught by "old maids" who were nasty, bitter, and sadistic. And made the picture on the Old Maid card game look like Scarlett Johansson by comparison.

If my son had had the Fourth Grade teacher I had, I would have home-schooled him, moved to another town, or had an attitude-adjusting chat with her in the parking lot with a tire iron.

Along with two boys, I was singled out for special abuse, Lord knows why. We're talking about a little 9-year-old girl here not some disrespectful teenager. I spent much of fourth grade with my head in my desk with books piled on top of it, or at the blackboard on my tiptoes with a circle drawn for me to put my nose in. (I have great calves to this day...)

Water-boarding would have been a welcome change of pace. Most of the infractions were allegedly for "talking in class." I must have been talking to myself, because nobody else ever got punished.

She's gone now, of course. Tried to outrun a train while driving drunk and it didn't work out. Oh dear. Holding a grudge is forbidden by the Jewish religion. So, to bury the hatchet, I have composed a posthumous Valentine to her: "Violets are blue; roses are red. I'm still talking, and you're still dead."

It's possible that "grudge" thing still needs some work.

To the rest of you dear Commenters, readers, and even trolls: Happy Valentine's Day! Tell somebody – kids, spouses, parents, mentors – you love them.

SPROUTS: or, Healthy as a Californian

September 12, 2014

My mother once sent me the dozens of warnings that came with her new Dustbuster including such useful suggestions as "Do not vacuum up water" and "Do not vacuum up burning ashes." The Nanny Staters who believe passionately in Darwinian Natural Selection seem strangely reluctant to let Nature take its course.

Go into any Ross Dress For Less store in California and prepare to be assaulted with signs every 2 feet alerting you to the fact that whatever you were planning to buy is fixin' to kill you. The California State Legislature is so overwhelmingly Democrat that there is never any danger of pesky debate, so what to do with their time? Clearly, the poor trough-diners have to think up ever more things to regulate and manage for your good:

That dress could cause cancer if you eat it! That butter dish may have lead in it! The Teflon in that pan could eventually come off and you could ingest it! RUN!

Mr. Ammo Grrrll and I just spent time on business in Solana Beach, California. The nearest market was a Sprouts, a delightful little place evidently aimed at the huge demographic of Californians who are terrified of their food. I went in search of some mayo and found organic, cold-pressed olive oil mayo with cage-free eggs. Shamelessly raised on Miracle Whip, I thought I would give this a whirl. It worked on a sandwich but Mr. Ammo Grrrll didn't like it.

I had had some childhood experience with free-range chickens. My Auntie Iva had chickens that you had to sweep off the kitchen table. There were chicken feathers in everything and chicken crap tracks across the tablecloth. It convinced me that chickens belonged in cages, or at least studio apartments.

Sprouts sells Baked Crackers in Crispy Sea Salt flavor which are not just gluten-free, but Xanthan Gum Free, contain no trans fats (rest easy, Mr. Bloomberg!), are ("proudly", yet!) Non-GMO Verified, suitable for Vegetarian Diets, and Nut Free!! However, they do contain milk, so lactose-intolerants beware! The crackers aren't bad for something made with "millet". But I miss the xanthan gum.

Did you ever notice how food purists keep raising the ante? Ammo Grrrll, for example, never knowingly eats baby seal or bald eagle. Of course, vegetarians eschew meat altogether. (They've never tasted my Brisket, poor babies.) Not satisfied with that, the vegans seem to say, "I'll see your no meat and raise you no animal products whatsoever." (I have seen articles that claim PETA-philes avoid wearing silk because the silkworm is exploited, evidently by not being paid $15.00 an hour minimum wage.)

Then some actress with a book to peddle says, "Well, I eat only RAW fruit and vegetables," as though cooking the carrots will hurt their feelings. Which is answered by someone who sniffs, "I don't eat anything; I only drink juices." And, finally, the winner is a 76-lb. woman who eats only twigs and berries she gathers by unicorn in the fairy forest. Our neighbor, the retired Texan, reported to us that last night he had a nourishing supper of Chocolate Vodka and Butterfingers. He weighs exactly what he weighed in high school. I don't. Do you?

Every decade or so, a new dietary paradigm appears to promise we can live forever. Mr. Ammo Grrrll has seized on a Power Line-linked article claiming drinking is good for you. He can't stop talking about it; at least I think that's what he's talking about. His words are kind of slurred.

Fat is bad – no, wait, fat is good; carb-loading is great; no, carbs are the tool of the devil; you might as well eat strychnine as sugar; and don't even think about gluten. The world is a disturbing place where almost everything is beyond our control. People want to feel they have control over something and, so, obsess over food. It is easier to control gluten than Putin.

You can feel free to pay twice as much for crappy-looking "organic" produce and scrutinize every mandatory food label. But, you still won't live forever. There, now I've gone and harshed your mellow. But, have a nice day. Try a doughnut; that always works for me.

GOOD ADVICE

February 27, 2015

I don't care if you are a sane person who understands that there are two, and only two, "genders," or more accurately, "sexes" (M & F), or if you are convinced that there are dozens of genders or none at all. It is – more or less – a free country except on college campuses, and you can believe what you want.

But if you are looking for advice on any particular topic, let me give you the benefit of some wisdom gleaned from my many decades upon this wacky planet.

If you want short, practical solutions to a problem at hand, ask a man.

If you want to just vent, or be listened to without even coming close to solving the problem, consult with a woman. In fact, there is substantial research claiming that that is precisely what women want when they ask a man about, say, a vexing issue at work. They just want him to listen; they do not want him to "solve" it. Further, it will even make the woman angry at the man if he tries to solve it. Talk about sandbagging someone!

So a woman (let's call her Gwynivere, since I've never known anyone by that name), will complain to her girlfriend, Lucille, that Judy at work is sabotaging her, taking credit for her work, and possibly even using her coffee cup in the break room.

Lucille will make good eye contact, listen intently and pat her hand and together they will discuss all the times they have been upset by coworkers. There may be tears; there may be hugs;

there will almost certainly be chocolate, possibly cocoa or herbal tea, and the ladies will feel much better.

Later that evening, Gwynivere might mention to her husband, Ralph, for the four- or six-hundredth time that she does not like Judy at work who is sabotaging her, taking credit for her work, and Ralph will sigh, look up for a nanosecond from online poker or ESPN and say, "As I see it, you can either confront Judy, or document your complaints and go to a manager, or you can quit."

There. Several different paths, each with different consequences. But, of course, Gwyn did not want ideas that would force her to act. She wanted sympathy. Ralph has made that mistake once again (doh!) and is mystified by her frosty reaction to his suggestions for certain activities later in the evening.

Obviously, there are exceptions to the general gender breakdown on this. No Mars-Venus paradigm is perfect. My women friends tend to be engineers, veterinarians, I.T. People, lawyers, data-driven, gun-totin' broads. While I love far-ranging conversation with all types of ladies, even the more touchy-feely among us, I do not enjoy beating any horse, but particularly a dead horse. Is that, by the way, not a thoroughly repulsive metaphor? I prize logic; love quick, practical solutions, and moving on in a sprightly manner.

And so, when my friend Angela (an engineer), who is a spectacular person though not a cook, asked me how long tuna salad would keep, I told her for sure 4 or 5 days with proper refrigeration. Now, as it happened, The Paranoid Texan was also on the patio when this conversation took place and he said, "Tuna salad will keep until it is gone." No slave to variety, the Paranoid Texan will fix a giant vat of tuna salad which includes hard-boiled eggs, and there's breakfast, lunch, and dinner for many days. Many.

This segued – as it naturally would while drinking – into a discussion of the proper way to fold contour (fitted) sheets. I said there was actually a YouTube video of the proper way to fold a contour sheet and that long before YouTube, my mother had attempted to show me how dozens of times to no avail. I further asserted that, unless the NSA is going to include linen closet inspection along with their electronic snooping (it's just a matter of time…), that just balling the damn thing up and stuffing it into the closet is good enough for me.

Once again, The Paranoid Texan offered the male viewpoint: "What folding? You take it out of the dryer and put it back on the bed." I said, "But I have several sets of sheets and I like to rotate them." And the PT, who is every bit as sensitive as he is paranoid said, "That's just stupid. You use one set till they wear out and get another set on Amazon."

It's hard to argue with logic like that even when sober. When Mr. Ammo Grrrll came out on the patio to bring out more bourbon, I informed him of the New Sheet Plan going forward and he said, "We have more than one set of sheets?"

INTERMEZZO: TRAVEL

I'm not a big fan of "confessionals." Anecdotes, yes. But working out one's psychological "issues" in front of an audience or in print, much less so. Nevertheless, I feel obligated to tell readers that I am probably borderline agoraphobic, if that word means anything close to "not wanting to leave my house, or even my recliner."

It's not that I FEAR going places, I just don't want to. Significant difference, in my opinion. As near as I can determine, this marked preference for staying at home emerged after thirty long years on the road, living out of a suitcase, and getting 4 am wakeup calls to get to the airport for a 6 am flight to East Overshoe, Mississippi. Where, for some reason, my agent always booked me AFTER Oregon or Connecticut. It was like she had a map and said, "What would be the FARTHEST point from here? Let's send Susan there next! With several connecting flights and a plane so small that even SHE has to duck."

My friend, Angela, and I have worked out a system much like the Homeland Security Warning System, only with numbers instead of colors. A Level 1 Trip involves leaving my home, but staying within the Gated Geezer Community. A Level 2 Trip takes me out the Guard Gate and to the wider Dusty Little Village with its useful grocery stores, donut emporia, and banks. Level 3 means I am obliged to go "to town" – primarily Chandler or Ahwatukee or Tempe – for dental appointments, Trader Joe's cookies and cereal, and Thai food.

Level 4 will take me into the wilds of Greater Phoenix for jazz or the Diamondbacks, or even all the way to Scottsdale, where I will always be inappropriately dressed and my $19 Walmart Fanny Pak will not fit in at all. Come to that, there really IS no place that the Fanny Pak is not the object of mirth and mockery.

Level 5 involves leaving Phoenix for other cities in Arizona such as Prescott or Winslow or Tucson or Tombstone. The stress of getting to any of those places is largely mitigated by the great food when you arrive. Heck, I would WALK to Winslow to eat at The Turquoise Room in the La Posada Inn. Barefooted.

Level 6 means leaving Arizona altogether, and once you hit Level 6, the discomfort level is pretty much all the same to me.

Long road trips seem less like leaving home than any other form of travel inasmuch as I take most of my home with me in my car. The Road Snacks alone take up the whole rest of the front seat.

This section could be sub-titled "Planes, Trains, and Automobiles", but I believe that is already taken. It includes a road trip, a plane ride, and a once-in-a-lifetime trip on Amtrak. Enjoy the journey!

HIGH SCHOOL REUNION PART 1

August 15, 2014

I returned to Arizona from a 5,000 mile, 17-day road trip back to Alexandria, Minnesota, for my – Krikey! – 50th high school reunion. My two best friends from high school joined me – Bonnie flying in from Minneapolis to Phoenix (after driving 2 days from Ontario!); Heather picked up in Ft. Worth, on our way north. They are twin sisters. Power Line readers will get many chances to hear about our Excellent Adventure, including local restaurants, the reunion itself, and a detailed description of all 1300 varieties of barbed wire in the Cowboy Hall of Fame in Oklahoma City with a quiz to follow: "Bueller? Bueller? Bueller?"

Bonus best bumper sticker: "Honk if you love Jesus; Text if you want to meet Him."

A road trip with me is bound to be an adventure because I have the worst sense of direction in the history of the world. I'm also seriously "dys-mapic." My forebears were probably navigators on the Santa Maria who "found" America when they were looking for the East Indies. My husband says I have a PERFECT sense of direction: I'm always wrong! Sadly, I cannot argue with this. Time and again on this trip we would be headed out of a restaurant parking lot with me saying, "Go right here, correct?" and Bonnie and Heather screaming in unison, "Left! Left!" Fortunately, all one needs to know to get from Phoenix to Minnesota (picking up someone in Texas) is 10 East til it turns into 20, to 35 North.

With three women of late, late middle age in one car, I worried that finding room for our luggage could be an issue. I begged, pleaded and cajoled to get my dear friends to pack "light." For this tiny, reasonable request, they called me "Bossypants" for the rest of the trip. Well, that, and my wanting to be in charge of everything. Sorry – firstborn; can't help it.

Clearly, "light" is in the eye of the beholder. I have seen women in airports with 7 pieces of matched luggage for a 3-day weekend. My sister and cousin and their saintly husbands once went on a day trip backpacking in the Rockies. The fellas thought that their packs felt a bit heavy, but soldiered on. Later it was discovered that my sister had packed a large cast iron skillet, and our cousin had packed the Denver phone book with which to press wildflowers.

Ammo Grrrll is something of an expert in packing light. I spent 30 years on the road for standup and usually had to shlep my own luggage. That'll learn ya right quick. Admittedly, my requirements are quite different from more normative women's: For example, I do not use makeup, which saves one large bag right there. Many years ago, an upscale department store tried to give me a "makeover" as an act of mercy, but I resembled an aging and none-too-successful hooker and washed it all off when I got home.

One of the twins – OK, Bonnie — had made a valiant effort to comply with the light luggage suggestion, mainly by dividing what would have been a mountain of stuff into dozens of small tote bags. But Heather brought out a suitcase that could have transported a smallish spinet piano and still had room left over for an alto sax. To the best of my knowledge, she did not have any actual musical instruments, more's the pity. But apparently she had included an anvil in case she wanted to do a little blacksmithing along the way to pay for the bowling ball packed next to it. It took all three of us to lift the bag into and out of the trunk. We definitely should have brought along a man.

Speaking of which, because we were Ammo Grrrll and a pair of twins, we called our road trip the Thelma, Louise and the Other

Louise Trip (TLOL for short). Search as we might, a young Brad Pitt never showed up to steal our money, possibly because of the six handguns between us, including a .357 and .45. But then, we didn't go over the Grand Canyon at the end either.

One of the highlights of our trip was shooting with John Hinderaker at his favorite range. Which was why we brought so many guns. He has previously posted what he called "the one target in which I beat you." Thanks, buddy! We fired a lot of rounds, so it was undoubtedly more than one. He is being gracious. John is an excellent shot, take my word for it.

Glenn, my shooting instructor, who teaches Law Enforcement Officers, has me practice almost exclusively with lifesize man-shaped targets from a distance of 21 to 75 feet. On most good days, I can make a nice two-to-three inch group in center mass, heads, and groins from those distances, with only a couple of fliers. For whatever reason, I am not as good with other types of targets like shapes and bullseyes. Be assured that should any of you be attacked by little green triangles or yellow circles, John has got your back.

Finally, I would like to thank all the lovely commenters from last week who, among other things, compared me to two of my humor columnist idols – Dave Barry and Erma Bombeck. My mission from Scott and John is to make y'all laugh or smile in the terrifying and depressing world that the rest of Power Line addresses. That so many of you respond positively is a source of great joy for me. God Bless You Every One!

And stay tuned for more about our trip next week.

HIGH SCHOOL REUNION PART 2

August 22, 2014

I believe it was French philosopher Alexis de Toqueville who said, "This is one big-ass country," but I could be mistaken. It might have been the Texan next door who likes Whataburgers and French Fries. An understandable confusion.

If you only fly over America – particularly her heartland – you can never really understand America. This country was meant to be traveled in a big-ass American automobile, or at least a mid-sized Korean one. It is darn near twice as far from Los Angeles to New York as from Paris to Moscow! Texas, alone, is just under 800 miles across.

On my recent 5,000-mile trip to and from Minnesota for a class reunion, with my two BFFs Bonnie and Heather, I got to experience those miles up close and personal. Before you get too old, tired or disabled to make the trip, I would highly recommend a leisurely jaunt across the heartland, stopping at whim to see what's out there. It is surprising and wonderful.

You have to be willing to engage with your fellow Americans, those warm-hearted and stunningly un-bitter clingers who just get up every day and make everything work. Most of what we discovered was serendipitous, one happy accident after another.

In a truckstop in Oklahoma, we chatted over terrific Barbecue with a Vietnam vet who had raised 24 foster children. In Guthrie, Oklahoma, we found a gorgeous giftshop called Aunt Gertrude's House. It was full of the most exquisite art, jewelry, scarves, and pottery. Though the lovely proprietor proudly featured only American crafts and art, she made an exception – out of support

– for Israeli artists! Who knew you could find a mezzuzah in a state known as the Buckle on the Bible Belt?

When I have journaled previous trips, most entries could be summed up in four words: "And then I ate…" Why stop now? The first night in Van Horn, TX, we found an outstanding meal at the historic El Capitan Hotel. The man next to us described his Chicken Fried Steak as the best he had ever eaten in his life. From my appetizer plate, I have no reason to doubt him. Bonnie's entree salad was a feast for all the senses.

If you read my post last week, you learned that I am directionally-challenged. And yet, I can find favorite restaurants on the road like a heat-seeking missile. In Big Spring, TX, where I had stayed on previous trips West, I fell in love with Albertos Mexican restaurant. Craving huevos for breakfast, we left the highway, and I drove right to its front door. Que cosa! It did not open until 11:00. With enough therapy, I may eventually recover.

In Wichita – both coming and going – we ate at P.F. Chang's. Though it's a chain, Bonnie and Heather had never experienced Chang's and we had an absolutely delightful waitress named Morgan. The food, libation, and service were exemplary. In a houseful of males (Household Motto: "The Seat is Always Up."), I have serious Daughter Deprivation and want to adopt every young woman I see. Morgan would make a good choice.

Got a world-class burger and fries at Retta Mae's Home Style Cookin' in Roscoe, TX. Retta Mae is an African-American lady and her staff and happy regulars of every race and color could have populated that "I Am An American" propaganda piece that ran tediously after 9/11.

We found the Holy Grail of Mexican food at La Posta DeMesilla in Las Cruces, New Mexico. My neighbor said he routinely drove there from El Paso for dinner, evidently because there's just not enough Mexican food in El Paso.

Guthrie, Oklahoma, was treasure trove enough to warrant another separate future trip. Ammo Grrrll normally has the patience of a teething toddler for museums, but The Oklahoma Territorial Museum is nothing short of delightful. My Daddy was a druggist and there is also an Apothecary Museum we will catch next time.

We left early enough in the morning from Guthrie to be able to hit the Cowboy Hall of Fame in OKCity when it opened. Ammo Grrrll had urged spending just two to three hours there in order to avoid the worst of rush hour when we returned Heather to Ft. Worth. Someone – why point fingers? – had squandered 30 minutes of that precious time in another slight directional error. (East, West – as HRC said, "What difference does it make now?") Besides, two hours at that Museum would be like two hours at the Louvres. There is simply too much to see.

In addition to 1300 kinds of barbed wire (barbed wire's greatest hits, culled from over 8,000 varieties), there is gallery after gallery of gorgeous Western and Native American art, a complete mock-up of a Western town, a vast collection of cowboy outfits worn in Westerns, a fine firearms gallery, a sprawling outdoor sculpture garden, a rodeo hall of fame, and an excellent lunch buffet! You quite literally cannot do it in a day. We spent five hours and the impending hellacious rush hour was totally worth it. (Photo below of the 3 amigas with Indian.)

And so we end this episode with Ammo Grrrll lost in the Beirut-like construction maze that is Dallas-Ft. Worth at rush hour. Going a restful 90 mph to avoid being rear-ended by Texans doing 100. And I did NOT run a red light. And never have in my entire life. It was yellow all the way through the intersection and the wretched "Safelight" camera photo that allegedly captured me must have been photo-shopped! A pro bono case for John or Scott?

Next week: the 50th reunion itself, or, "Who are all these codgers?"

HIGH SCHOOL REUNION PART 3

August 29, 2014

You know those beautiful young ladies in high school back when you were a nerd who could never date them (if you were a boy) or BE them (if you were a girl)? Well, they are still beautiful! What kind of karmic fairness is that? Some of them look like they just stepped out of Miss Skalbeck's English class on the way to the lunchroom. (It's meatless Friday, so it's either Fish Sticks or Mac and Cheese, back in the quaint old days when a Christian religion was modestly accommodated.)

So, that's the bad news. The good news is that by age 67 or 68, the old cliques have pretty much broken down. By this reunion, people had stopped trying to impress each other and circulated nicely, talking to everyone. Heck, we're all just geezers now who have done our best, accomplished much, and are hoping that when we meet Our Maker, many years from now, He grades on a curve.

Out of a class of around 240, 175 people registered for the reunion, including some spouses and teachers. There were no nametags at our opening cocktail reception. Some people were instantly recognizable. Others could not have been guessed if my life had depended on it. Whatever reunion you attend, do NOT say, "Guess who I am?" This can only lead to embarrassment all around. Just stick out your hand and say, "Hi, I'm Somebody Johnson" (in Minnesota), or "I'm Tammylou Faye-Anne Whatever" (in Texas).

A dear, late friend of mine told me that when her father visited his native Czechoslovakia, then still Communist, he ran into an old woman whom he recognized from gradeschool and broke the ice after 50 years by asking, "Don't the government give you teeth?"

Better openers at your reunion would be neutral sports talk: "Would soccer be tolerable if limited to one two-minute shootout? OK, how 'bout with actual guns?" or "Should they change the name of the Golf Channel to The Cialis Channel based on the number of commercials for it?" What's up with that, so to speak?

I am blessed to be one of very few people my age with two living parents. I had to divide my time between reunion events and parental visits, so I left early. The next night was our big banquet and dance. I sat with travel mates Bonnie and Heather and a guy who still had a crush on Bonnie and Heather who was livin' the dream for one evening.

This time we had nametags with our senior pictures on them in case we hadn't been humiliated enough in life. Whatever made me think a Lilt home perm the day before pictures was a great idea? It may be an urban legend, but I read that Barry Manilow bought up all existing copies of his yearbook and destroyed them. If I ever get that rich, count on it!

The organizers of the reunion had done a bang-up job with the banquet. It opened with the Pledge of Allegiance, led by a career Army classmate. The dance band then played all the military anthems for every branch of service and had the vets who had served in each branch stand to sustained applause. It had to be over half the men in the class, God Bless 'em. Bonnie, who is a veterinarian, also stood by mistake. OK, I made that up.

Colleen, the emcee, recalled that a certain strict English teacher once scolded a periodically-disruptive student thusly: "Susan, your life would go much better if you didn't think you were so funny." Rumor has it that her life went just fine. So, neener,

neener.

After the banquet, the cover band played the music from the Sixties. Ammo Grrrll was a dancin' fool for over an hour. The next day everything hurt, including my hair.

Finally, it was obvious that none of us had gotten through life without challenges and sorrow. No matter how successful, how financially secure, everyone I talked to had dealt with something – from disabled children to mental health issues; from surviving breast cancer to broken marriages and addiction. Life can be a marathon through a minefield.

We are here not to see through each other, but to see each other through. Our class was good at that. Many thanks to the organizers. On to the 60th. This time we'll leave more time for the Cowboy Hall of Fame even if we need three walkers then instead of just the one.

COME FLY WITH ME!

October 31, 2014

Even before Ebola, Ammo Grrrll only flew under extreme duress. Funerals. Emergencies with sick parents. For business, I have DRIVEN from Minnesota to West Virginia, Maryland, and Texas. I enjoy long road trips. There is nobody to complain when you play the same Toby Keith disc for 3 hours, followed by Brahms' Second Piano Concerto and then *The Best of Bread* ($1.99 in a bin). Eat your heart out, Brahms. Here comes "Baby, I'm-A Want You".

Flying itself is wretched enough, but nowadays the TSA Experience begins the fun. It apparently is my karma always to be singled out for the full wanding and gunpowder residue tests on my hands. Tests I am terrified I am going to flunk because of the frequency of my shooting, despite Lady Macbeth-level scrubbing.

But who could blame TSA for culling me out when you consider the many hijackers who have been short women comics born the same year as Cher and Dolly Parton? Just as long as we don't "profile"; that's all I care about. And what the hell is "profiling" anyway, but the rational practice of giving extra scrutiny to those most likely to commit a particular offense? Why is that wrong? I would hope that when a white serial rapist is loose, that the police don't waste valuable time and resources investigating a lot of black women.

And why the heck couldn't that jackass shoe bomber have put the bomb in his hat instead of his shoe so that we all have to take off our shoes now for the next umpteen years? I forget what religion the guy was – Episcopalian, maybe? Not that his religion was relevant in any way. Motive unknown. Again. Probably toilet-trained too early or something.

Part of my problem with flying is that I have an insufficient faith in both gravity and engineering. I believe that the only reason the plane stays aloft is the exertion of my massive will. If I let my guard down even for an instant, it could spell disaster! The other passengers so seldom indicate the slightest gratitude for my vigilance. A nod, a salute, would be nice.

I try to use points to bump up to First Class because if the plane does go down, at least I will be having a free drink. My last flight I had picked up the mail on my way to the airport and had my latest issue of *American Rifleman*. When I got to the airport, I bought *People* in order to lower my IQ by 30 points and also to hide my NRA magazine inside it away from TSA's prying eyes as they pawed through my carry-on after the traditional wanding.

Seated next to me on the plane was a sweet, clean-cut young man who looked in frank disbelief at the (late, late) middle-aged lady reading NRA's magazine while enjoying an adult beverage. He grinned, handing me a business card, and informed me proudly that he designed and sold moving targets for a living, mostly to police training facilities. What are the chances? We talked guns n' ammo all the way to Minneapolis.

The festive bumper stickers on the first car picking up a passenger outside Lindbergh Terminal were for gun control, Diversity (Celebration of), the late Paul Wellstone, the lame losers Kerry/Edwards, and Obama/Biden. Twice. And the despicable Edwards wasn't even scratched out! Was this lady driver against anything, you ask? I mean, since she obviously was fine with a man cheating on his dying wife, making a baby, denying the baby's existence until caught, and exploiting rich old doddering campaign donors? Well, yes, as a matter of fact she was "Already against the next war." You know, to save time.

Ah, the Twin Cities, just as I remember them. Come for the windchill; stay for the brain-dead politics. C'mon, Minnesota: surprise us this Tuesday! See how many Republican ballots you can find in the trunks of your cars.

AMTRAK AND ME

November 28, 2014

Mussolini, it is asserted – undoubtedly falsely – made the trains run on time. Benito would have hanged *himself* if tasked with running Amtrak.

Several years ago, when we were still wintering in Palm Springs, I decided to make the annual journey south into a four-day "Bucket List" train trip adventure. Pat, a fellow writer and Certified Train Nut, promised it would be a ball. Mr. Ammo Grrrll opted to drive. Mr. Ammo Grrrll is a very smart guy. I swear every word of the following description is true.

For the nominal sum of $1,000, I booked a First Class Sleeper Cabin the size of a double-wide coffin. It had a tiny "sofa" bench that turned into a tiny bed. It had a tiny toilet. It had a tiny shower, accessed by sitting upon the tiny toilet. Kind of a full-body bidet. The only available route was St. Paul to Chicago. Disembarking. Staying overnight in Chicago. And the next morning continuing on from Chicago to Palm Springs. Convenient!

Having watched *Murder on the Orient Express* and other movies which glamorized train travel, except for the murder part, I envisioned exchanging pleasantries with international sophisticates while dining on Pheasant Under Glass served by slim waiters wearing gloves.

So I have to confess to being a little disappointed when the first wretched meal was lukewarm microwaved chicken and nuclear TaterTots served by portly, unsmiling unionists. We were herded into the limited-space dining car in shifts, given no choice about menu or dining companions, and encouraged to eat quickly so as to accommodate the next shift.

My first dining companions were three massive women traveling together who spent the entire meal reliving their recent colonoscopies in vivid detail and eyeing my uneaten Tots. I was beginning to understand how someone could get murdered on a train.

I have failed to mention that this was over the Thanksgiving weekend. Can you guess who spends family holidays alone on a train? Crazy people, that's who. Permanently in residence in the bar car was a tattooed woman who volunteered that she was in AA , NA and a support group for Sexual Addicts. The trifecta of bad life decisions coupled with an imperfect understanding of the word "anonymous". There were seven empty beer bottles in front of her. This was a new, relaxed rule for AA with which I was not familiar.

Beside her was a rail-thin woman on her way to California to marry a man she had met once on a hiking trail. Having known me for well over 10 minutes, she invited me to the wedding. With them was a young man they had just met who seemed to be hanging around the self-confessed sexual addict in hopeful anticipation of a relapse there as well. God willing he had packed a Hazmat suit or at least Kevlar condoms.

For three endless days I read many books, listened to my iPod, ate the apples and Protein Bars I had brought, thanks be to the Almighty, and tried to get some exercise by walking the length of the train. It's tough to go very fast down crowded aisles in a lurching train.

When we changed crews in San Antonio, the train was left unguarded in the railyard overnight! There are no locks on the sleeping cubicles which makes for a restful night without a firearm. At least we exchanged our surly Chicagoans for some polite, friendly Hispanic Texans. I was happy to be shuck of the sullen guy who turned my sofa-bench into a bed each night. Clearly, he had been wearing his uniform for months while playing raquetball. Turned out I could hold my breath for longer than I thought.

A fun and surprising fact: freight trains have the right-of-way over passenger trains! Who knew? Repeatedly we had to sit on the tracks for hours at a time to accommodate them. In Palm Springs at last, they dumped us in the middle of nowhere in the desert where I kissed the unmoving ground and called a cab. Any day now I plan to speak to Pat again.

This Thanksgiving was ever so much better with my husband safely back from Israel (Baruch Hashem), and a wonderful meal with beloved friends in my beautiful Arizona. There was not a Tater Tot in sight.

INTERMEZZO: POLITICS AND PC

The Power Line site on which I am given a guest platform every Friday, features three very smart lawyers and one smart AND funny academic. It covers cultural and intellectual issues, but mostly politics. The trouble with politics is that the shelf life is notoriously short. Therefore, on occasion, I will throw in a word or two of explanation before the columns so that readers can understand what the heck the issue even was that had me all wrapped around the axle at the time.

One good thing to remember going through Life, is that issues that loom large and all-consuming at the time are almost as fleeting as the more minor kerfuffles.

I am old enough to remember (vaguely) the Kennedy-Nixon debates in which a sweaty old guy with a five-o-clock shadow debated a young, handsome guy with a funny accent. At least, that's how I remember it. I was 14, what else would I have noticed?

Anyway, a major issue in the debate concerned the fate of two islands in the South China Sea called Quemoy and Matsu. I do not personally remember which candidate took which position on this burning issue of the day – Mr. AG asserts that it was Kennedy who insisted the U.S. had to defend the islands -- but I am dead certain that neither Quemoy nor Matsu was ever heard from again. I expect that both will eventually be baby names, perhaps with a D'La in front of them.

My point is that some of the issues addressed in the following set of columns became as obscure as Quemoy and Matsu within a week. So, maybe we should all just relax more instead of freaking out. Other issues, of course, reverberate still and will seem "ripped from today's headlines!" You never can tell what will endure. I gave Rap Music a month when I first heard it some thirty years ago, give or take. My parents said the same thing about Rock 'N Roll. And Mr. AG predicted that Madonna's big coffee table book on "Sex" would be a flop. So, maybe neither one of us exactly has our finger on the pulse of cultural trends.

Nevertheless, the following columns represent my reactions to various and sundry political issues of the day. I hope you enjoy revisiting the issues and my take on them.

BOSSY

April 4, 2014

With contrived controversy and manufactured outrage flying at warp speed, I am often late to the party. So, I know I'm behind the curve on the Bossy meme. But I've got some time waiting for the Holy Grail of .22 LR – CCI Stingers! – to come out, so I'll weigh in anyhow.

The list of degrading terms for women, the utterance of which can get you read out of the human race, is extensive. Many are understandable – the wretched "c" word; the slightly-less horrific "b" word, slut, skank, ho (unless you're a rap artist).

First they came for those nouns. And Good Riddance.

Then they expanded the list at dizzying speed to include the mildly offensive, the benign, and the frankly puzzling: broad, chick, girl, gal, ladies, (yes! Ladies!) and so on. This led to hilarious articles in radical 60's newsrags in which little 12-year-old girls were referred to as women. Which probably came as welcome news to Jerry Lee Lewis, Woody Allen and Roman Polanski.

Alas, your old-fashioned country gentleman Dad could not stop using "ladies."

And clueless Mom just outright refused to give up "coffee with the gals." Poor Mom who bore six kids and worked in a defense plant and knitted mittens for the troops and planted a Victory Garden and canned her own vegetables, and was always chosen first for sand-lot baseball – well, she just didn't have

TIME to realize what a downtrodden, politically incorrect, embarrassment she was. She didn't even realize she was an Entitled Victim!

And now, they've come for the adjectives.

Womyn celebrities, far richer and more important than you, have declared that female persons of any age cannot be called Bossy. Ever again. Just in time for Hillary's second run. (Sadly, last time pigment trumped plumbing.)

Evidently, all little girls and even highly-paid female executives cannot be called Bossy without crushing their fragile egos and squelching their leadership potential. In fact, there is no such thing as a Bossy woman or pre-woman, even if one of the bossy celebrity scolds is hellbent on forcing school lunch-ladies to offer nothing but Lima Bean and Liver Surprise with a side of Kale.

My old Irish grandpa used to say, "You throw a stone into a pack of dogs, and the one that barks the loudest is the one you hit." Is there a chance that someone who objects to being CALLED Bossy, actually IS Bossy? Is there a chance that where there's smoke, there's a big fat raging fire?

Perhaps we could settle this with a working definition of "bossy"? Well, let's hear it. And if bossiness exists, why in heaven's name can it not apply equally to males and females?

In the real world, there is such a thing as "leadership" – a platoon leader who leads by example, by not asking others to take risks he or she is not willing to take, by making sure everyone knows you've got their back; Or an executive who seeks input from others, draws out the shy person, doesn't demand credit, but does take responsibility.

And then there is Bossy: insecure, imperious, quarrelsome, demanding, ungrateful, pompous, nasty. Riding roughshod over others. Enjoys humiliating people and ordering them about. And guess what? We know the difference.

If you don't know bossy people of both genders (she said heteronormatively), then, like the President, you haven't ever had a job. The best and worst boss I've ever had were both women. One was brilliant and hard-working; tough, but fair; demanding perfection and modeling it; asking much, but expressing appreciation. A Leader par excellence. She served for decades.

The other was petty, lazy, dishonest, incompetent and mean. And those were her good points. She was also bossy. She lasted a few months.

BRANDEIS

April 11, 2014

Sometimes in the course of soliciting donations, taking meetings, golfing, taking lunch, speaking on the phone, the busy college president must make a controversial decision.

Doncha hate when that happens?? Yikes, how to proceed?

Let's say you are President of Brandeis University. Some chucklehead decided to acknowledge the unimaginable courage of a woman who, at great peril to her life, fights to shine the light of public opinion on the plight of untold millions of oppressed women.

(No, no, not the women who can miraculously afford another tattoo or hair extensions or weekly nail appointments, or extra cell phone minutes, but need to have somebody else, anybody else, come up with nine dollars a month for free birth control. Clearly, anyone suffering that level of oppression would be too traumatized to speak a word.)

This is Ayaan Hirsi Ali, a beautiful Somali woman whose enemies are the people who behead human beings and then upload their feats on YouTube for the viewing pleasure of millions of their fanbois. They throw wheelchair-bound Jews overboard on ships, murder Ms. Ali's artist friend in the Netherlands and slaughter people in broad daylight in Jolly Olde England where, thank God, at least potential targets are not allowed to carry defensive weapons.

Then let's say that a jaw-dropping 85 employees at your

institution protest honoring this woman and allowing her to address the graduating class. Yikes! What's a man-shaped substance to do?

A. Fire the 85 employees. It's a tough economy. Surely you can find 85 professors who understand the concepts of free speech, and actual diversity?

B. Blame the Koch brothers.

C. Crumple like a cheap aluminum walker when hit by a semi.

Congratulations! You correctly chose "C". Now, in coming up with a reason why you can't find your balls with a tweezers, you claim:

A. Because War on Women. Oh wait, this IS a woman. Try again.

B. Because Raaaacism. Oh crap, she's also black. Try again. (Good Lord, she also has high cheekbones. Puh-leeeze don't let her feel like she's an Indian, too.)

C..Because we weren't aware of how much she clashed with our core values. No need to explain what your "core" values are. As Groucho famously said, "These are my principles. If you don't like them, I have others."

Once again, you have chosen C. Good answer! The media won't touch this with a ten-foot pole, and soon Lindsay will be back in rehab or Miley will twerk, or Kim will be pregnant with little South, and who will care about some African nobody who probably isn't even gay?

Rest assured if you HAD allowed her to speak, The Slavering Mob would have shouted her down, but talk about a buzz kill for a graduation!

TRANSGENDERS IN THE MILITARY

May 16, 2014

So now, the Obama Administration feels that – of all the problems we face foreign and domestic — we must "pivot" urgently to address Transgendered people in the Military. Is there NO grown-up in the room? Has he reconstituted the Choom Gang?

The Military is not a door prize at the Entitlement Banquet. It is an elite fighting force to keep us safe in a perilous world. The Range Officers at my gun range are almost all ex-military and a fitter, leaner, group of gentlemen would be hard to find. Awesome shots, too.

Of all the entities that the Diversity Crowd believes "should look like America," the Military is dead last on the list. America, in the main, is old, female, and fat. Characteristics that don't come to mind for storming beaches in Normandy.

Speaking of which, I demand to be made a Navy SEAL! True, I am a short, weak woman of extremely late middle-age who can't swim. But to deny me this honor is sexist, age-ist, and non-swimmer-phobic. I plan to be the first dog-paddling SEAL. In a life jacket with a Water Aerobics Noodle. Hoo-yah!

Is it possible that a particular Transgendered person could be a good soldier? Of course. So what? And anyone who can make the grade without being shoe-horned in because he/she fits a protected category could be considered. In spite of being Transgendered, not because of it.

Let me tell you about just one Transgendered person's story told to me (without names, of course) by her physician.

We have a person born a woman. She can have sex with men or with women, even marry them. Unsatisfied with such limited choices, she elects – undoubtedly on either the taxpayer's or insurer's many, many dimes – to become a man, with all the hormones and various surgeries that entails. She grows the obligatory silly little goatee. Life should be good.

If you think we're done now, you would be mistaken. Does she want her lady bits back? That has certainly occurred too, but in a way, it's even more bewildering. Several months later, she decides – wait for it – she's a GAY Man! Yes, you read that right. So now, instead of having sex with men with the equipment she was born with, she's still having sex with men, only with fewer, uh, options. Well done! Is this the mark of mental stability in a person you would welcome fighting next to you?

Since I'm already way in the deep end of the politically-incorrect pool – without my Noodle – let me ask this: could someone please explain to me how the Transgendered are an oppressed group anyway? I do understand that in the transition phase a person could come in for some funny looks, even bullying. But that phase would be of short duration. And, obviously, bullying is always wrong. But why the eternal entitlement?

If a lifelong man (Oppressor, Male Privilege and all that) VOLUNTEERS to become a woman, how would he be any more entitled to privilege than if I went around in blackface in order to get Affirmative Action?

And if a Woman (Oppressed, Downtrodden, #WaronWomen) becomes a Man, has she now not changed sides in that war and become worthy of all the opprobrium heaped on our husbands, sons and brothers?

And when, dear God, can this fragmented Balkanized country ever again just look at MLK's "content of our characters" and not worry about whether we have a wise, diabetic Latina, a straight Irish rich man named Kennedy, or a transgendered black bisexual in the Army, the Navy, the Village People, or on the Supreme Court? It cannot come too soon.

WHOSE TURN IS IT?

June 13, 2014

Well, we've had our first Black President, which is working out splendidly. If her supporters have enough time to come up with even one accomplishment, and her extensive wardrobe of unfortunate pantsuits still fit, Hillary may be our first Woman President. Zippa-de-doo-dah. And we can hear about the fabulous historic historical wonderment of it all for many months until the First Gentleman boinks another intern, this time a guy to atone for signing DOMA into exceedingly temporary Law.

The notion of nomination by category is offensive on the face of it. MLK's dream that people be judged by the content of their character and not the color (or shape) of their skin has turned into its opposite. Now pigment and plumbing are everything. If, in the wretched past, 1/16th black "blood" made one black, it is now a point not only of pride but of privilege. Heck, you don't even need to prove your racial bona fides. Just FEELING that your cheekbones are high and that makes you a Cherokee is enough to land a coveted teaching position and be mentioned as a possible First-Runnerup Substitute Woman should the Low Information Voters be persuaded that a Benghazi is not a fancy sports car.

Can you imagine that it won't even take until 2020 for the Perpetually Furious Grievance Crowd (PFGC) to demand a Gay President? A Hispanic Vice President? And why just a regular old boring gay person? That's offensive to the Transgendered – the gay president should be a former man, now a woman, who is a lesbian. And why should the Hispanic Vice President be a citizen? How unfair to the undocumented! (assuming by then there are any undocumented left who haven't been made voting citizens).

Asians and Jews never count to the PFGC. I once was asked to entertain at a Diversity Conference in Minnesota that these ultra-sensitive, diversity-celebrating, tolerance-teaching folks scheduled for Yom Kippur, the holiest day of the Jewish year. You can bet your bottom dollar they all knew when Ramadan was.

But we haven't had a Jewish President, an Asian President, a Navajo President, or, for that matter, a Polish President, Italian President, Czech President, Syrian President, Disabled Bisexual President, Hearing-Impaired Transvestite Haitian President, or Large Samoan Lesbian President, to name but a few "under-served" categories. Let's make a list of all the people who fit into these categories and then put their names in a hat for a random drawing. What's the difference if we are going for category and not qualifications or politics?

It goes without saying that Dr. Ben Carson, Condi Rice, Sarah Palin, Ted Cruz, Marco Rubio, Susannah Martinez, Mia Love need not apply. It is a well-known fact that conservatives fit into only one category: H8Rs. One Professor Wendy Doniger said in the 2008 campaign, "Palin's biggest hypocrisy is her pretense that she's a woman." So that leaves us with one more category which Ms. Doniger can fill nicely: she could be our first Blind Jealous Vicious Ninny President. But mostly Blind.

IT'S THE END OF RACISM!

June 27, 2014

Many years ago, Albert Brooks wrote and starred in the wonderful movie *Lost in America*. Briefly, a highly-paid ad executive and his ditzy wife chuck the high life to go on a quest to discover America and "to touch Indians." Hilarity ensues. But early in their adventures the wife loses their entire nest egg in Vegas. An apoplectic Brooks explains that since she cannot understand "the nest egg principle," she will be forbidden from even SAYING "nest egg" or any part of "nest egg": "You will have to call a nest 'a circle of twigs,'" he says. This came to my mind as I read the reports of tens of thousands of unaccompanied minors being dumped in America on spec to cash in on prospective amnesty. Huh? Bear with me.

How many times have you tuned in to a news network panel discussion on "comprehensive immigration" only to hear some frothing La Raza hacktivist accusing opponents of raaacism, of simply hating all brown people? La Raza means "the race." (THE Race? Haven't we tried this before? Does Master Aryan Race ring a bell?)

Well, this obviously-coordinated Children's Crusade means game over on the racism accusations. **A country safe enough for busloads of brown children is not racist.** Would a Guatemalan mother not be scared to death for her little brown children if she believed this? Clearly, she KNOWS America is not racist. The trick is getting TO America through a phalanx of cheating, lying, brutalizing, raping, thieving, murdering "coyotes" who happen to be the same color as her children. Like a horrific game of Human Frogger.

As a Jewish parent, I see dozens of countries on several continents to which I would never even ACCOMPANY my child, let alone have sent him there without me when he was young. Heck, I wouldn't even send a Jewish child to Presbyterian summer camp now that their bigoted, leftist crapweasel leadership has passed "divestment." But that is for another day.

So either the tedious race-baiters of The Race have to ADMIT that this is one of the few countries on the face of the earth that can be counted on to try to feed and shelter their little ones until this travesty is sorted out; OR, they have to admit that these are horrible parents to deliberately send their children into the belly of a racist beast.

So is America good, or are brown parents monsters? Pick one. And if they say that the kids are not coming to be Tot-Squatters for Amnesty, but are just desperately fleeing gangs and poverty – right this minute, curiously, after generations of poverty –then, once again, what COLOR are the exploiters and beheading drug dealers in those countries?

The beleaguered American taxpayers of all colors (but majority white), will attempt to deal with this wholly-manufactured "humanitarian crisis." I never want to hear the word "racism" in regard to this issue again. In fact, when a Professional Race Card-Dealer from The Race is on the next panel, he or she should not even be allowed to say any part of "race." If they want to talk about a hundred-yard dash, they should have to say "a thing where people run fast to cross a finish line." Ya basta! Enough!

LIAR or IDIOT: YOU BE THE JUDGE

July 18, 2014

After the *Hobby Lobby* Supreme Court decision, Indian Princess Elizabeth Warren peered over her high cheekbones and tweeted the following 25 words: "Can't believe we live in a world where we'd even consider letting big corps deny women access to basic care based on vague moral objections."

A mere 25 words with a minimum of four fallacies or lies. Yikes! Let us list them, shall we?

She begins with the mistaken belief that the Supreme Court has jurisdiction over the "world." This is completely consistent with the hope of the far-left that we will someday have to take our marching orders from Brussels or the U.N. Sadly for them we still live in an independent country, not "the world."

Notice how she also mentions we shouldn't "let" corporations do things. This is also a central tenet of the Left and applies not just to corporations, but to people who like large drinks or mothers who like to pack a lunch for Junior that he will actually eat. People much smarter than you know what they can let you do.

Secondly, there is the rather hilarious term "big corps." Ah, yes, a closely-held corporation consisting of five religious family members is a "big corp."(not to mention the world-beating Little Sisters of the Poor in their lawsuit). Warren is a lawyer. She knows better. The Hobby Lobby store is big, so that might have confused her.

In Hollywood, outside of the occasional Christian Fanatic Nutjob, the go-to villain in everything from cartoons to re-writes of The Manchurian Candidate is always the Evil Corporation. There is no other kind. In the original movie, the villain was communist. That is so yesterday, what with the Reset Button and all, that sadly for the Ukrainians turned out to be a Rewind Button instead. Oopsie!

In Left-wing La-La Land everyone should either work for The Excellent Benign Government or sell puka shell necklaces to each other (if you can comply with the 4,000 pages of Puka Shell Necklace regulations.) Failing that, Nancy Pelosi suggests writing poetry, an apparent high-paying growth industry.

Thirdly, there is the Big Gigantic Histrionic Steaming Pile of a Lie that is repeated like a mantra: that if someone else doesn't pay for your birth control, it is exactly the same as "deny(ing) (you) access" to it. Jim Crow all over again!

For the love of God, Lizzie and gal pals, get a grip! Take a Valium or do some Tai Chi. There is no woman in America who cannot afford $9.00 a month for birth control pills and condoms are free at any gay bar. Especially if a woman shares the cost with her husband, boyfriend, hookup, or Baby Daddy, then that unbearable burden falls to $4.50, or the price of a cup of coffee. Nothing to the individual, but quite a sum indeed to the taxpayer in aggregate.

And, finally, there's the assertion that Hobby Lobby's successful lawsuit was based on "vague moral objections." There was nothing the least bit "vague" about Hobby Lobby's moral objections: they did not want to pay for procedures that snuff out the life of an unborn child, even in its earliest stages. Period. You may disagree with it, but how is that "vague"? The ruling exempts Hobby Lobby from paying for only a handful of the many birth control methods, the ones which are abortifacients.

This tweet is an embarrassment to my gender. And yet, Warren is bandied about as a credible back-up candidate for First Woman President, a person to carry on the "legacy" of Obama.

Oh, she would be that, alright. If the legacy is a wildly-unqualified, one-term leftist senator, filling a politically-correct slot, who has lied about his or her background for personal gain. Never forget that the original "birther" was Obama himself. For 18 long years, he let stand his bio saying that he was born in Kenya. That sounds so much more exotic than a pot-smoking private school punk born in Hawaii, the most racially-tolerant place on earth.

Does anyone doubt that the reason his college records are sealed is because he got special consideration based on this lie? If not, unseal them, already; I'm sure they've been redacted by now. Or lost in a hard drive mishap. In Ms. Warren, we have yet another fake Indian who was listed as a "woman of color" at Harvard, that color being Fish Belly White. She let that stand, too. At least as a Bankruptcy specialist at Harvard Law, she could preside over the remnants of Obama's economy as it circles the drain.

SCHADENFREUDE

September 19, 2014

Many years ago, when I still had to navigate the Minnesota highways in winter, I had one of those experiences that fall under the category of Schadenfreude. That is, of course, a fancy word for taking unseemly pleasure when someone is hoisted on his own petard.

Petards being in short supply generally, my first Schadenfreude involved a car.

After a couple of terrifying spin-outs, one with my 3-year-old baby in the car, I admit that I was a very cautious winter driver. On this day, we had icy, blizzard conditions, and I was driving on the freeway in the hinterlands. A red Corvette was tailgating my slow-moving little Saturn, honking and giving me the finger in a very un-Minnesotan manner. The approved method of indicating driving dismay in Minnesota is to pull even with the offender, make eye contact, and shake your head slowly while clucking your teeth.

The guy would not let up. Though I was in the right lane, he was clearly demanding that I drive faster and refusing to go around me. After many scary miles of almost touching my bumper, he pulled around in fury and gunned it. I had nearly pitted out my down coat and was very happy to see him go.

Not five miles down the road I saw just the top of a red Corvette buried in the right-hand snowbank. I'm pretty sure the Christian – and definitely the Jewish – thing to do would have been to stop to offer assistance. But, it was only a few short weeks until Spring thaw, and I didn't want to ruin his teachable moment. I'm confident he couldn't hear the giddy laughter over Merle Haggard singing about always being on a mountain when he falls.

The second memorable Schadenfreude event happened in the Ritz Carlton hotel in Naples, Florida. My room was not ready when I checked in. They apologized profusely, and I was waiting patiently in the lobby, sipping on the third tropical drink that was supplying the patience.

At last, the front desk clerk motioned for me to come up to the desk to get my keys. Before I could get there, a furious young woman pushed ahead of me, nearly knocking me over. She was dressed in designer clothes from head to toe. Her purse and briefcase cost more than everything in my closet put together, including the exercise bike behind the muu-muus. With no offense to Scott, John or Paul, I'm pretty sure she was a young lawyer. She was waving the room assignment she had in her beautifully-manicured hand.

She harangued the desk clerk in a loud imperious tone: "I clearly informed you that I wanted a room on the water when I made this reservation! This is completely unacceptable. How can you people be so incompetent?? You have put me on the golf course!"

And the desk clerk replied in that icy, yet courteous tone mastered by gay men: "Madam, ALL our rooms are on the water. We do not have a golf course. That room is on the Gulf."

Oh Lord, I wish y'all had been there. Sadly, this time my laughter was not covered by Merle. If looks could kill, your humble humor columnist would not be alive at this time.

And so, this brings us to the present day and Barack Hussein

Obama, mmm, mmm, mmm.

He is still our President, the only one we've got, and Commander in Chief in what may or may not be "war"-time, depending on the spokes-tool or the definition du jour of "war" or "terrorist" or "Islamic." Bill was only unsure of the definition of "is." Clearly, this whole crew needs a good dictionary.

When I think of the way that President Bush was treated by a sniping Mr. Vote Present and the left-wing of his party with the towers still smoking on the ground, it is really hard not to feel some measure of Schadenfreude that The Ocean Lowerer is being swamped by events. You can take months to decide which puppy most reminds you of the lapdogs in your press corps. You know they will wait forever, tails wagging, legs twitching, with their little reporter's notebooks in their teeth. But you cannot dither forever acting on intelligence to rescue a hostage without disastrous consequences and "bad optics."

I clearly remember a discussion in the letters section of the Minneapolis paper about whether it was moral to hope for America's war plan to succeed if it meant that the Evil "Bushitler" – gosh, what cleverness! – would get credit for it.

I'd like to think that our side is better than that. Or at least better than me.

KATY, BAR THE DOOR!

September 26, 2014

When I was a child living in a small town in rural Minnesota, we rarely locked our doors, certainly never when we were in the house.

My husband grew up in suburban Chicago where they locked the doors at all times, which I found irritating and downright rude. How can the neighbors walk in unannounced to borrow sugar or shoot the breeze if the doors are locked?

The first home we owned as young marrieds didn't even HAVE a lock on the back door for seven years. We had almost nothing worth stealing. Not to mention the three cat boxes which acted as nasal tasers.

Times change; eventually we bought a decent core door with a deadbolt lock. To Mr. Ammo Grrrll's annoyance, I often still forgot to lock it when I was home alone. To my much greater annoyance, he locked it when it was twenty below zero outside and I had groceries to bring in. Oh, the fun of biting off frozen mittens to grasp a metal key while your husband reads an article in the warm, cozy bathroom! Who's out doing home invasions at twenty below?

Now we live in our Dusty Little Village (DLV) in Arizona, recently rated 7th safest in the state. Our home is in a Gated Community of Geezer-Americans. So, our first line of defense is a corps of laughably unfit, unarmed security guards. The main job of this crack security team, besides discouraging the most inept of adolescent miscreants, seems to be patrolling the neighborhood to make sure we don't put our garbage cans out too early.

More usefully, we have expensive security doors on all entrances, doors that my shooting instructor, himself a sheriff's deputy, has assured me are – and I'm quoting here — "a bitch to breach with a battering ram." Mr. Ammo Grrrll and his tag-team nagging partner, the Paranoid Texan next door, insist that I lock the door, even when I go out to water the flowers.

So, you can imagine my astonishment that Mr. Omar Gonzalez, alleged White House intruder (or "undocumented badge-less visitant"), just sprinted right in the front door to the White House carrying a puny little knife.

Yes, by now everyone knows: THE DOOR WAS NOT LOCKED!! Que? It's a darn good thing no Paranoid Texan lived at 1602 Pennsylvania Avenue! That would never have passed muster, boy howdy!

Since the First Family was away, maybe the Secret Service wanted to make it easier for the hookers to get in. But, no one shot Mr. Gonzalez or even shot at him. No dogs were let loose, not even Bo, who was probably at Camp David with the family.

Mr. Gonzalez was under indictment in Virginia for possessing a sawed-off shotgun and a tomahawk. In his car, he had a machete and two hatchets. He had a map of the White House and also — why not? — of the Masonic Temple. Plus 800 rounds of some kind of ammo.

He is very lucky that his name is Gonzalez and he is not the dreaded "white Hispanic." He looks just like Obama's son, if Obama had had a son when he was around 9 years old. Mr. Gonzalez is allegedly an Army vet, possibly with PTSD. His family says he "meant no harm". We will hear very little more about him, except sympathetic stories mentioning racism, poverty, George W. Bush, the hell of war, and other exculpatory information.

But, can you imagine the endless uproar had his name been Bubba Joe Jasper, just a garden-variety "craven hillbilly" veteran who – God forbid! – had once been to a Tea Party rally? MSNBC and CNN would have had to treat their seven viewers to a special logo — a teabag in a KKK hood? –- featured on the hourly updates from now until the election. Of 2016.

Mr. Gonzalez will disappear into the ether with the Mohammads and Hasans and various other inconvenient offenders who committed "man-caused disasters" or "workplace violence." (Who knew "Allah Akhbar" was Arabic for "Take this job and shove it."?). Remember that Muslim soldier who threw grenades into the tents of his fellow soldiers? No? Neither do I.

If Mr. Gonzalez is a disturbed vet, he will probably get treatment in a facility where, presumably, they will lock the door. Maybe the White House will too.

THINGS I SHOULD HAVE SAID and ONE I DID

October 3, 2014

Last year I found myself in a fancy Palm Desert resort when a well-dressed woman with a San Francisco address on her convention nametag approached me. Did I know any good restaurants? I suggested Peppers, my favorite Thai place. But I misunderstood what she was getting at. "No," she said, in a tone you would use with a slowish child, "Not good like that – CLEAN." "Well, the food is the best Thai I've ever had, and the bathroom is spotless."

"Not clean like that – clean food! My husband eats so clean, you should see him when he comes down here – he looks years younger than his age."

I did not say, but should have: "You should see my mother. She made me brown sugar sandwiches on Wonder Bread. Her lard piecrust is the flakiest you will ever eat. She always cooked with a crock of bacon grease she kept under the sink. Did I mention she's well on her way to 94 and looks to be somewhere in her late 70s?

Many years ago I was tired of being overweight, and determined to lose 20 lbs. (Again.) As usual, I succeeded. During that small window between thrilling success and inevitable relapse, a woman who had not seen me in awhile came up to me at an event and said in a very loud voice: "Oh my Gawd, you've lost a MILLION pounds." Yes, that's right – not a hundred, not a thousand, but a million pounds. And I did not say, but should have: "You hit the nail right on the head! You should be a weight guesser at the Fair! Yes! I have lost exactly a million pounds and now I can move from the Grand Canyon back into my home."

My mother is a very frugal lady, tighter than elm bark. She was raised dirt poor in the Depression. She thinks any homemaker who does not mix up her own juice from concentrate is a hopeless spendthrift. She will water down condiments until the day when you have Lake Ketchup all over your burger, your plate and the table. She has never thrown out any food. At a restaurant, she has been known to ask for a to-go box for half a chicken wing and two peas. She frequently will approach a family member with a Tupperware container whose contents are only lightly-tinged green and say, "Here, eat up this beef; I think it's going bad."

To which I HAVE said, "Oh boy, give me a big plate of that Beef Going Bad, Mama. How do we know we got it in time?"

The last private gig of my standup career before retirement was in front of teachers at their late August in-service before the start of school. I was the final speaker of the day. I had listened to many administrators and the Keynoter who was a Diversity Drone from the state. She seemed a nice, sincere person, even though she arrived forty minutes late for her speech keeping hundreds of people waiting. There was probably a diversity emergency somewhere.

The main thrust of the entire day's remarks had been that there was an achievement gap between the white students and the students of color as they are called today. (Thank God it's not the bad old days when they were called colored students). SOMETHING – the teachers, society, racism, poverty – was responsible for this gap! Definitely not the students themselves. Gap, gap, gap, gap, gap. They were FAR more concerned about the GAP than about everyone's simply mastering the material, perhaps by — oh, I don't know – studying harder. Or at all.

There is a certain delicious freedom in knowing the gig is your last. I entertained the crowd and then ended with: "I have an idea. Since it's the GAP between the white and minority students that you find so upsetting, why don't you just encourage the white students to do WORSE?"

There was a brief stunned silence and then the room burst into laughter and applause. Maybe there is some hope yet for our country.

GIFTING AND REGIFTING

November 7, 2014

This column appeared the day after the Republican success in the 2014 mid-terms, what Obama referred to as a "shellacking."

Tuesday night put Ammo Grrrll in an unusually festive mood. And that is why God invented Excedrin. God Bless America and the observation attributed to Lincoln that you can't fool all the people all the time. I was beginning to think Abe had it wrong. The election feels like a gift and hence our topic today.

With the holiday season just around the corner, and Christmas accoutrements up in stores since August, "Gifts" is a good topic, election or not. Giving and receiving gifts is a lot more complicated than it would seem at first blush. In several cultures, gift-giving involves subtle protocols which the unwary could easily violate, causing hurt feelings, misunderstandings and disaster.

Hillary's idiotic Red Restart Button springs to mind. Or The Lightbringer's jaw-dropping gift to the Queen of England of his own droning speeches. In a format that doesn't work in the UK.

Luckily, he made up for the crappy gift by returning the Churchill bust. Maybe he'll give the Statue of Liberty back to France, too. He's more of a fan of "redistribution" (def: n.. looting) than liberty. That torch could leave a carbon footprint, and Lady Liberty should probably be wearing a nice polyester pants suit instead of a hetero-normative dress. ("Give me your poor, your tired, your huddled masses with a low-grade fever, willing to self-quarantine part-time except for bowling…")

My sister is a kind, lovely person with elegant, particular taste in all things. When designing and furnishing her house, she took days to select the unseen slides for the kitchen drawers. My sister's husband jokes that for her birthday he gives her a "ceremonial" gift and the receipt, because, inevitably, it is going back.

Far less elegant or particular, I had my Mexican handyman pick out the paint for my walls. The house is very bright and gay in the original meaning of the word. I would include a picture, but The Paranoid Texan Next Door claims the colors sometimes frighten the unprepared. Think Sunshine Yellow, Green Tea Green, and Periwinkle! Yes, witty Top Commenter Arnold T., it's a real color – kind of a lavender blue.

If you want a quick lesson in humility, try writing a little humor book and finding not one, not three, but FIVE personally-autographed copies on your synagogue's used book sale table. Several somebodies had given them as gifts to people who had been underwhelmed.

Since the names were in the books, I was sorely tempted to buy them up and surprise the owners by wrapping them beautifully and returning them. With yet another autograph. ("P.S. Resistance is futile. This book will find you wherever you go.") Then I remembered my favorite t-shirt: "The cops never think it's as funny as you do."

And then there are greeting cards. What a racket! They were a quarter when I was growing up, fifty cents for a big, fancy one for your Mom. Now, they can cost dang near as much as the gift. My thrifty friend, Randy, hates cards and just requests the extra $3.50 in cash.

My favorite-ever greeting card story comes by way of my friend,

Linda. Linda worked with a woman whose unemployed middle-aged son still lived at home. The mother waited on him hand and foot and he was not even nice to her. Talk about Failure to Launch!!

On Mother's Day when she opened the card he had tossed at her, she realized that he had run into the convenience store when he got up at noon, grabbed the first card he had seen without reading it, and signed it with just his name.

She figured this out because the card read: "You've been like a mother to me."

Oh God. If you don't think that's funny, there is truly no help for you.

PLANET DIVERSITY

December 12, 2014

We didn't get T.V. until I was 12, and except for sports, I just never really took to it. Mr. Ammo Grrrll makes up for it, though. Either the T.V. is on or he's not home. Oh, some programming is decent; but, I find most commercials since the retirement of the E-Trade babies unbearable. And would die happy if I never heard about erectile dysfunction again. Or puzzled over the bizarre outdoor twin bathtubs. What part of that looks sexy? Do they have bunkbeds, too?

When I was a kid, a deodorant commercial couldn't even show the human armpit, which was considered unseemly. They showed statues, specifically, the Venus de Milo, who didn't have arms, much less an offensive odor. Now there's a blonde British babe prattling on about how erectile dysfunction happens to all men sometimes when they're with their "honey."

During the World Series, I saw a commercial featuring a young black homeowner who was extremely fond of his Dodge Dart. His neighbor, a cretinous white guy, kept trying to scratch his lovely new car with garden tools. The jerk's motivation for this is a mystery. My African-American neighbor owns a nice Mercedes. Should I approach his car with a leaf-blower or pruning tool, I would expect to get shot. And deserve it. He is retired military.

As obnoxious and unrealistic as this Dodge commercial is – and, yes, I GET that it's supposed to be edgy and humorous (Lololol!) – here's the point: Never on this earth will you see the reverse in a commercial. On Planet Diversity, no white homeowner will ever be accosted by a tool-bearing black guy trying to harm his car.

Ever.

Neither will any commercial for a home security system feature a crew of black home invaders. All the homeowner has to worry about on Planet Diversity is a plague of ugly white criminals in hoodies. To portray any black man as a criminal in a commercial would automatically be racist. With hell to pay from the Dynamic Duo of Rabble-Rousin' Reverends.

Pay real attention to the commercials for just one night instead of making a sandwich. You will quickly notice there is an heirarchy of correctness for commercials on Planet Diversity.

There is equality of one sort: Married men of all races are hen-pecked morons whose wives are much smarter and more attractive. The pathetic idiots never know what cereal to eat or which laxative to use. It's a miracle they can dress themselves and locate their jobs.

Black people are always cooler, smarter, and hipper than white people in commercials. Any doofus will be white. The guy with the "wrong" phone or computer will be white and uncool. Black people can be cutely wacky, like the football player who gets excited when his number comes up at the deli. But they can never be stupid, bad, ugly, or subservient.

Asians do not exist except very rarely as part of the wallpaper in a crowd scene and identifiable Jews do not exist at all. Any women who are "acting stupidly", will also be unattractive. An example is "Helen" the bad dancer at the high school dance where JJ Watt appears. But in most ad "storylines", women will be thin, pretty, and in charge.

Children of all races are smarter than adults, but particularly their fathers. Father not only no longer knows "best"; he knows next to nothing. He is lectured by his offspring about phones, computers, cars, and his own investments. Without kids to tell him what's what, he would be probably be homeless. Once again, played for humor, but part of the relentless assault on everything male, traditional, or authoritative. Government is Big Daddy, Sugar Daddy, and Baby Daddy now; no need for any real flesh-and-blood fathers.

No matter how many other tribal subgroups are featured in the future, straight white men will still be the idiots and bad guys, so embrace it, my brothers. And don't even get me started on the portrayal of Christians in network programming. It's a national disgrace and would not be tolerated with any other religion, including wiccans or practitioners of voodoo.

JONATHAN GRUBER

December 19, 2014

I grew up in the Fiber-Free Fifties. With a steady diet of Jello, Trix, Wonder Bread, and Velveeta, small wonder laxative ads were prominent on television. Housewives discussed the issue openly in commercials, usually with their pharmacists and often volunteering that their husbands who were standing right there, humiliated, also had issues with regularity. One popular remedy was Ex-Lax, a product that masqueraded as a chocolate bar, and one that many many children sampled. But only once.

In truth, even disguised as a chocolate treat, the taste was a dreadful disappointment, even to a toddler. We weren't really very fooled. But by then it was too late. I imagine that some marketing executive was paid a handsome sum of money to come up with the idea of making it look like candy. And if a few hundred thousand children spent a day chained to their potty chairs, well, a small price to pay to sell more product.

Fast forward to the early 21rst century. With Hillarycare a dim memory, the Left became urgently concerned once again about the "uninsured." It was a crisis, we were told. The system was broken! Why, there were upwards of 40 million people without health insurance! Dying in the streets, they were. Yes, not even in their own beds, but staggering into the streets! Russell Brand said so, and inasmuch as he's never had an original thought in his life, he was not alone.

Never mind that the uninsured included among them millions of people who made over $75,000 a year and just didn't find health insurance a very sexy thing to buy when you could just show up at the ER for the flu or a broken arm and they had to take you in.

Another large percentage included people who qualified for Medicaid but were too lazy or uninformed to apply for it. The young and invincible didn't want to pay for it when they could get another tattoo instead. Yet another large component were, of course, illegal aliens, but the U.S. Taxpayers were called heartless for refusing to provide platinum health care coverage for all of Mexico. Just for starters.

Enter Jonathan Gruber and his co-conspirators with both hands out to Grub in the bottomless government money trough while trying to make the one-size-fits-all steaming disaster that is Obamacare work its way through the body politic. First, make the plan many thousands of pages long so that nobody, even serious policy wonks, could read it or make sense of it. Second, make it impossible for the CBO to score it accurately. On purpose. Third, ram it through on strict party lines with no input whatsoever allowed from the other side. Trot out heart-rending examples of what happens to people without insurance, and allow no unseemly digging into the actual facts of the narratives, not one of which held up to close scrutiny. Are you calling that sweet little orphan boy's dead mama a liar?? Bribe, wheedle, threaten, strong-arm. Repeat.

But, mostly, lie through your teeth. You can keep your doctor or current insurance: wink, wink, nudge, nudge. It wasn't a tax! Hell, no. Until it needed to be. Death panels? Sarah Palin is a lunatic. Grant thousands of exceptions to the more onerous rules to your homies. The lying had to be done, doncha know, because the American people are just too slack-jawed stupid to understand any complexities. Did YOU go to M.I.T.? I didn't think so. Me neither. With all the lies to chocolate coat the process of moving the bill through the system, Nancy Pelosi was more prescient than she knew when she said we had to "pass the bill to see what's in it."

One thing that has become apparent with the left wing is that they are just terrible winners. When a single gay judge in California overturned the defeated gay marriage referendum, which itself was back on the ballot in defiance of the previous overwhelming defeat, it wasn't enough to win. People who had opposed redefining marriage, even years previously, had to be punished, including with loss of their jobs.

And it wasn't enough for Jonathan Gruber to help provide the chocolate in the Ex-Lax to make Obamacare progress smoothly. It wasn't enough for him to walk away with tons of "street cred" for future consulting and wheelbarrels full of money. Enough money that he would never need to "work" again. (Please, God.) Think of that — set for life.

No, he had to taunt. He had to brag. He had to chortle about the knee-slapper he put over on us rubes. Never mind that that's yet another lie – it never had majority support in polls. Maybe from the usual beneficiaries of freebies, but not from actual taxpayers footing the bill. We weren't fooled. Like the kid with the crummy chocolate Ex-Lax, it was simply too late. Is there no remedy to recoup any of our money from these criminals and liars? The Solyndra thieves, the multimillionaires at the top of the Fannie Mae food chain, the "hide the decline" frauds in the global warming bidness? John, Paul, Scott, anybody? I'm just a retired comic, not an attorney, but isn't deliberate, admitted fraud still a crime?

A LIFE FULL OF MICROAGGRESSIONS

December 26, 2014

Sometimes I think my life's story could be called "A Life Full of Microaggressions." What with "The Audacity of Hope" already taken and all. And it would be the same for every hapless human. I will mention a very few "slings and arrows" from my life. For example, In 7th grade I brought my adorable six-year-old sister to a school basketball game and a cool girl classmate said, "That's your little sister? But, she's so cute! She looks nothing like you." Ouch.

Now, it's true that I've never suffered the racist horror of being asked to reach something on a high shelf, as First Lady, Mrs. Obama claimed. The great novelist, Lee Child, who is 6'6", got the name for his protagonist when his wife told him if this writing deal didn't work out, he could always be a "Reacher" in supermarkets, so frequently was he asked for help. Me, only if elves are shopping. And very short elves at that.

I have countless times been mistaken for a Walmart employee by customers of every hue. And I've never once thought to be insulted by it. In the summer when it's 117° outside, I walk at Walmart. So, when people see a lady without a cart, striding purposefully, they think "employee." Still, it's odd, because even in Arizona, Walmart's uniform does not include an "I Carry a .9 Because A Cop Is Too Heavy" t-shirt. Yet.

Except for .22s, Walmart's ammo shelves are now full, but a year ago when I stood in line every day, I had the following micro-aggressive encounter. The new ammo was supposed to be out by 7 a.m. When it wasn't, I asked the young lady in Customer Service to please page the manager. Over the P.A. System I heard, "Nate, that old lady who is always here for ammo wants to talk to you." Moi! A woman of late, late middle age was called "old" by a Mexican youngster. Outloud! I am a very, very good Walmart customer. I probably could have gotten her fired if I were a thin-skinned, giant d**khead. Liberals love to get people fired. Conservatives like people to have jobs.

But I had been called old before. When I was 25 years old, I was taking karate in San Francisco and I lost the spare key to our apartment at the dojo. I put up a little note on the bulletin board about it. While I was changing into my gi (uni), behind the lockers, I heard a little gaggle of adolescent Asian girls reading the note, "Who's that?" one asked, and another replied, "That's that old white lady." Just a pale crone at 25! Naturally, I sued the karate school, the teenage girls for racism and the makers of the gi for good measure. Not.

Could I ever have taken offense because of my religion? Oh, my. Once on a plane, I had ordered the kosher meal, and the well-dressed lout next to me looked up and out of the blue, said, "You people have to get over the Holocaust." He is very lucky indeed that the silverware was plastic. It was a long, silent flight. At a minimum I could have asked to be reseated because I didn't feel "emotionally safe." Truth to tell, I was hoping he would make a move so I could strangle him with the oxygen cord. Was that wrong?

And once, many decades ago in New York City, waiting on the corner for my husband to pay the tab in a diner, I was approached by a very icky man who took me for a hooker. I wore no makeup, and had on tennies, jeans and an old flannel shirt that just screamed hooker. Wasn't that more insulting than being mistaken for a valet as President Obama mined his entire life for at least ONE instance of racist oppression? I don't frequent places that have valets, but the few times I have, they have all been fit young men who run for the cars.

But, perhaps, my most hilarious "dis" occurred early in my career. A do-gooder working with Shakopee Women's Prison called and begged me to entertain – for free, of course. Many of the ladies there are of color. I booked the date, even turned down paid work later for that date. One day before the event, the lady called. "The women don't want your little skit", she said. "They voted for square dancing instead." Yes, that's right. Not bumped from The Tonight Show because a much bigger star ran over his time. Bumped from doing "my little skit" for free in a women's prison. Is there no one I can sue for that? Al, Jesse, little help here!

Millions of African-Americans raise families and get up every day and work without complaint or inventing grievances. I could name 10 at my local Walmart alone. To those other African-Americans who see "raaacism" in every human encounter, I say this in love and sincerity: I have been insulted and demeaned for my age, my sex, my religion, my profession, my height, my looks, my politics, and my race by the whole Rainbow Coalition. It is called Life, lived among disappointing, imperfect, sometimes-cruel human beings. It happens to everybody. You just aren't that special. Get over yourself.

A microaggression is just that: micro. On second thought, instead of "A Life Full of Microaggressions," my life's story should be called simply "A Life Full." I am blessed beyond any possible sense of merit. People who look for offenses with a magnifying glass: Count your blessings. Start appreciating and enjoying your life. You will be a much happier person.

Next week the discussion continues in "Microaggressions go to college."

January 2, 2015

Last week Ammo Grrrll took up the question of microaggressions in A LIFE FULL OF MICROAGGRESSIONS. The question of microaggressions has taken shape on campus, where sensitive souls face mortal peril every day. It only makes sense that Ammo Grrrll returns this week with

MICROAGGRESSIONS GO TO COLLEGE.

In the Autumn issue of City Journal, the brilliant and brave writer Heather Mac Donald, lifted the lid on the lunatic asylum that the modern campus has become in her treatment of "microaggressions" — the teeny tiny unintentional insults and nonexistent to minuscule offenses we discussed last week. The article is long, detailed, depressing, and a devastating indictment of academia's kowtowing to the Perpetually Aggrieved Entitlement Crowd.

Capitulating to these disrespectful, willfully ignorant, gibberish-spouting thugs in college will lead to a conveyer belt of similar ideas into the workplace as surely as God made little green apples. It is readily apparent that the fewer actual obstacles women and people of color have to success, the more that have to be made up out of whole cloth.

When I read about the eggshells that today's professors have to walk on to avoid giving any offense to the fragile, yet belligerent Snowflakes, I think of my flamboyant and wonderful college French teacher, Madame Gaumer. She would have melted a few Snowflakes. I could not forget my first day of French II class at Northwestern University even if I had had a full frontal lobotomy. ("I'd rather have a bottle in front of me than a frontal lobotomy." Rim shot.)

In those days, when dinosaurs roamed the earth, if you waited for 10 minutes for your professor to show up to class, you could leave. At precisely 9 minutes after the hour, a reed thin "woman of a certain age," smoking a smelly Gauloise cigarette, wearing 6-inch heels and a tight leather skirt, blew through the door, hair flying. She was speaking rapidly in a language I thought must be Italian, as I did not recognize a single word, despite having taken what I was pretty sure had been two years of French in high school. I had been advised to enroll in college French II rather than the introductory course.

"Okay," I thought. "I will sit here as quiet as a mouse (*comme tranquille comme une souris*) as I am obviously in the wrong class, and flee at the end of the hour, never to return." She began taking attendance and speaking to each individual at some terrifying length. Uh-oh.

Despite fervent prayer, a meteor did not hit the classroom. She called my name and asked me a question. My mind was a Magic Slate. I tried to intuit which phrase I remembered could possibly be the correct answer to her question: "The pen is on the table," or "Margot and my uncle are going to the library." What were the chances that she gave a crap where the pen was? And why, come to that, did my uncle spend so much time with Margot?

"Evidently I do not speak French," would have been the appropriate answer. I was too traumatized to speak at all and feared I might either throw up or cry, neither an attractive option, even in a 17-year-old.

She must have made fun of me because the rest of the class, made up of her previous French I students, laughed heartily. In retrospect, I'm pretty sure that was a microaggression or possibly even a mini-one. Since she was a Parisian, she routinely mocked students for speaking with a South of France accent. What is it about the South in every country that elicits such condescension? She also clearly preferred the boys over the girls and flirted openly with the guys.

After that disastrous first class, she took me aside and explained that I should probably drop the class and re-register for Beginning French I. She said my only other alternative was to work really, really, really hard to catch up to the upperclassmen. She didn't hold out much hope for me. I said the only other thing I could think of: "I have a headache, but sometimes it snows." And then I resolved to work hard. Really, really, really. And did.

While my roommate (Drama major, legacy, astonishing binge drinker) went to fraternity parties, I stayed in our dorm room translating Proust (great) and Camus (overrated, depressing). I sat with a French-English dictionary on one side and a regular Oxford dictionary on the other, since often, even after I found out what the French word meant in English, I still didn't know what the English word meant. It took me hours to do a short lesson from a wretchedly boring book called *Village en Vaucluse*. And then one day, *Mon Dieu!*, I was actually speaking French! (Bonus old joke: Beautiful coed goes to professor and says, "Sir, I will do ANYTHING to get an 'A' in this course." Professor: "Anything?" Coed: "Yes." Professor: "Try studying, dear.")

I made respectable, hard-earned "B"s for three quarters – years before grade inflation – and with a prodigious effort, made an "A" the final quarter. I have rarely been prouder of any accomplishment. And so, Mme., wherever you are in your 80s or 90s – an iron lung or a Left Bank apartment in Paris with your 50-year-old lover – I thank you for not coddling me, for making me earn the right to "esteem" myself. *Merci beaucoup*. The microaggrieved should be so lucky.

COMPARATIVE VICTIMHOOD

March 13, 2015

We Americans are just naturally competitive. I don't care if Little League doesn't keep score; the kids know who won. (And God Bless the Ten Run Rule without which we'd still be there.)

One Sabbath long ago our rabbi told this little parable, which I must paraphrase from memory since I have no idea where he got it. If I am infringing on copyrighted material somewhere, I apologize in advance.

A young man became enchanted with Eastern religions and meditation. He went to live in a commune of like-minded individuals with a guru. He wrote back to his parents: "I have spent the first part of my life competing for grades, competing for scholarships, competing in sports, competing in music. Now that I have rejected all those material trappings, I have found peace of mind. We eat simple vegan foods and meditate all day." And then he closed with:

"P.S. With sustained practice, my guru believes I can be the best meditator in the commune."

People will compete about anything. Listen to mothers talking about childbirth: "I was in labor for 15 hours without an epidural." "Really? My twins were born breech at the same time, and I was in labor for three days." Here's Jewish ladies talking about Passover Seder prep: "You're having 42 guests? That will be so cozy! We've invited 112. I've been boiling and peeling the eggs for the first course for 2 days. Sam is building an addition on to the dining room."

But no competition is more determined than Vying for Victimhood.

In the early days of The Movement, it would be generally agreed that Black Women had it pretty rough. But then ideological camps would form on who was more oppressed Black Men or White Women? The political arguments were fierce, if patently ridiculous.

Most of the people involved in these discussions were trust-fund wastrels, Red Diaper Babies (people whose own parents were Communists), limousine liberal professors, and work-averse idiots in their 20s (self-described "community organizers") who had never been "oppressed" for even a day in their lives. But becoming part of a Protected Class turned out to be very lucrative. Why, you could become a Harvard Law professor just with imaginary high cheekbones in your round fat pale face!

Then new categories of victims were added, seemingly daily. What about a gay Black man versus a disabled Hispanic woman? What weight to give what alleged obstacle? Transgendered was far in the future. And now that glorious future has arrived!

Pass the popcorn, indeed. We have Germaine Greer, godmother of the early feminist movement, author of *The Female Eunuch*, going on about her, uh, sorry, fellas, I'm quoting here, "big, smelly vagina" and saying that "females" without one don't count. (Smelly, really? Good Lord, woman, I know you're European, but have you thought of a daily bath or shower? It's remarkably effective.)

Heaven help us. This decades-long yapping about vaginas is so tedious. We've had vagina art. We've had chatty vaginas engaging in monologues. I'm just grateful vaginas apparently only talk to themselves and not to each other. That could be awkward in a business meeting. Though I suppose helpful on, say, the Bar Exam: "Pssst...Little help here...what's the Rule Against Perpetuities again?"

And now with Greer's claim that "women" without vaginas aren't really women (duh!), the vitriol unleashed against her has been mind-boggling. She has joined pariahs like Condi Rice in being disinvited from speaking engagements.

The most hilarious example of a combo plate of Competitive Victimhood paired with Barry's "No Matter What You've Done, America is Worse Project" was when he went to China. He felt pressure to briefly mention a flagrant human rights violation there and then offer his standard escape clause: Sure you torture and imprison dissidents, but Asian-Americans in the U.S. suffer discrimination, too, because..uh, uh, oh, yeah, because they suffer different rates of some digestive cancers. Yes! That's what he came up with. Really.

Of course, he couldn't tell the truth about the worst discrimination Asians face, which is that after years of studying and pushing from their Tiger Mothers, their perfect grades and high test scores count for spit (as Steve Hayward documented recently). Dollars to doughnuts Barry himself took the place some Asian-American had earned. Heck, maybe my own son did, since Asians need even higher test scores than people of pallor. It's very important to penalize the people who study the hardest. Check your privilege! Not everybody can study, y'know. Oh wait, yes, they can.

I say if 75% of Asian-Americans voted for this avowed redistributionist, then my sympathy is limited. The Admissions Office just redistributed 300 points from your daughter's test scores to somebody else! Hope she enjoyed all those violin lessons and advanced calculus classes.

ONE YEAR ANNIVERSARY

March 27, 2015

Hey, fans, Top Commenters, trolls and friends! Guess what? This is the First Anniversary of Thoughts From the Ammo Line! The first column debuted on March 30th, 2014.

I had been standing in the ammo line at Walmart for hundreds of hours over the year-long ammo drought, with plenty of time to chat with the other shooters and to fill the long hours with anecdotes, political discussions, jokes of questionable (OK, bad) taste, and lots of gun talk. As a woman, in the arts, from Deep Blue Minnesota, and Jewish to boot, by rights and demographic stereotype, I should be a gun-hatin', Obama-votin', social justice warrior.

But — and I know this comes as a surprise to regular readers — I'm not. In fact, the night Obama was elected in 2008, I was so upset that when Ohio and Indiana (Et tu, Indiana?!!) electoral votes went to Obama, I drove most of the night to be in a Red State on my way from Minnesota to wintering in Palm Springs. I had to go all the way to Oklahoma, where not only did the state go Republican, but every county did. Mr. Ammo Grrrll, who would fly out to join me later, went to an Election Night "party" with other non-Obamabots. When people asked "Where is your wife?" he said, "Gone. To a Red State, she said." "No, really, where is she?" "Gone. Really." Ammo Grrrll doesn't take disappointment well.

When two years later, we moved to Arizona, and I became an avid target shooter, it occurred to me that the two friends I had at Power Line (John and Scott) might be interested in a humor column from that perspective. Power Line had been my go-to sanity keeper for nigh unto ten years. (And what a debt of gratitude we all owe them!) It was particularly fun when John fell in love with shooting too.

I emailed my introductory column to Scott just to see if he was maybe, possibly, interested and within – as The Gropester would say — "literally" — three minutes, he had posted it! Oopsy daisy. Be careful what you wish for; you just might get it.

That was fifty-two columns ago, give or take. (Without a doubt, a commenter will count them and they may only total 51.) Frankly, I don't know how the Power Line boys do it, three, four items apiece a day, because one a week is tough enough for me.

I am very fortunate to hang out with a number of witty people: Mr. Ammo Grrrll, The Paranoid Texan, Angela, Bonnie, Heather, and others. When comics hang out, they are very guarded about coming up with too many good quips lest your fellow comics say, "Hey, that's funny. You gonna use that or can I have it?" With my friends, whose professions don't require an endless supply of good lines, I feel I have carte blanche to just shamelessly steal anything funny they say. In exchange, I provide my World Famous Deviled Eggs, Awesomely Good Chili, Melt-in-Your-Mouth Brisket, and a casserole so wonderful Angela calls it Turkey-Crack Casserole.

My motto: Will cook for funny material. And also provide liquor.

One of my great life lessons is that everything – and I do mean everything – is harder than it looks. Especially as a guest columnist on somebody else's site, I try very hard to hit "center mass" every time. But, in life, as in target shooting, sometimes you spray and pray.

To say that I appreciate the support of you commenters would be to understate the matter considerably. Thank you so much for your kind words. Sometimes in standup, people would come up to me and compliment me on my set and then say: "I bet you get tired of hearing that, huh?" To which I would always answer, "No, actually, we don't." I'd like to list my favorite commenters but the list would be long and I'd be afraid of leaving someone out.

And so, on we go to the next 52. I hope to continue to brighten your Fridays. The only downside of a once-weekly column is that I can't always be terribly current. Forgive me. I had a really funny (IMHO) Top 10 List of Reasons Why Obama Didn't Go to Paris written on a Sunday, but by the time Friday rolled around (particularly slowly that week it seemed), other columnists, bloggers, and even witty commenters had come close enough to most of my jokes to make them look stolen and stale. I asked Scott to sub in a different column. Oh, well. Civilization will survive without that piece.

Oh, also, my goal is to really get in shape this year and exchange the ancient photo by my column with one of me in a gun porn pose like Steve puts at the end of his awesome Week in Pictures post. (A crane shot from sniper distance.) I don't look exactly like some of those ladies, but at least I could demonstrate proper gun safety. It has come to my attention that very few of you gentlemen even care that the lady is often exercising very poor trigger discipline. Crikey, sometimes you don't even notice she has a gun. You might change your mind if you were in front of her; but then, from what I know of men, you might be willing to take that risk and just die happy.

INTERMEZZO: GUNS

Sometimes when I write a column about guns, I get something wrong, a couple of times hilariously so. The gun experts will leap on me like a World Series team leaps on their winning pitcher. And I have to remind them that – despite my nickname, given to me by the salesclerks at Walmart – Ammo Grrrll knows relatively little about guns per se. And probably started way too late to ever know very much except how to make the things go bang.

There are ladies featured in *American Rifleman* and *Guns 'N Ammo* who are extremely knowledgeable. Usually, they are about 40 years younger than me and quite a lot more fetching. The great, lovely, and heroic Dana Loesch comes to mind.

The title of my column is Thoughts from the Ammo Line. But it could just as well be Thoughts from the Office Supplies Line or Thoughts from the Doughnut Line. If there were a deliberate (or coincidental—haha, right!) shortage of either office supplies or doughnuts and I wanted to make sure that I got some of the scarce few, then I would stand in those lines, just like the poor blokes in the former Soviet Union. They would get in ANY line, just IN CASE there was something at the end of it, like a roll of sandpaper-like toilet paper, or one semi-rotten egg.

But it happened to be ammo that was in short supply in 2011-14. So, I became an expert at standing in ammo lines. What you mostly need is a lot of patience, relentless persistence, a fair amount of money, and a great deal of time on your hands. In other words, the perfect description of the retired comedienne and mediocre housewife. Eventually, I also got to know the sweet young Hispanic Mormon who unloaded the big Walmart trucks overnight and he would text me if there was any ammo on the truck. Many days there was none.

I became friends with a whole bunch of guys who truly ARE gun experts, in one case, an Army vet and private contractor who spent five years in combat in Iraq and Afghanistan. Except for the fact that he is an excellent husband, father, and grandfather, and is also much saner than any Democrat politician, his collection -- which rivals Charlton Heston's -- and his encyclopedic knowledge could qualify him as a gun "nut".

What I mostly want to say about guns is that we were gifted by our forefathers with the right to keep and bear them. Those much-maligned "old white men" (or freakin' GENIUSES, in my humble opinion) who signed the Declaration of Independence knew a thing or two about tyranny. When you observe how the average Deplorable WITH GUNS is treated by the powerful, swampy State and its totalitarian-loving defenders, just imagine how we would be treated without them.

Verily, every single subsequent right – freedom of press, of speech, of religion, of assembly – is only guaranteed by the freedom to keep and bear arms.

Yes, guns are also critical to protect our lives and property, and are used to that end somewhere in America each and every day. As the perhaps trite but completely true bumper sticker goes, "When seconds count, the cops are just minutes away."

But, mostly guns protect and defend our rights and way of life.

Make no mistake. The Left in this country aims to dismantle every right and sacred principle in this Republic and now they aren't even embarrassed or reluctant to say it aloud. If they ever get back in power, Obama's "redistribution" plans will look like a minor tweak to our way of life.

Buy a gun. Take a safety course and learn how to use it.

AMMO IS SCARCE

April 18, 2014

After my first post, Responder Pete Parks (Salisbury University) said, "Finding ammo is a pain." *Es verdad, Pedro, es verdad!* Bilingual Arizona talk for "Yes, Pete, it's true!"

But, fear not, for Ammo Grrrll is here to tell you all you need to know about succeeding in the difficult world of scarce ammo: Find someone who already HAS ammo and offer to pay double for it or to put a hurtin' on 'em unless they share. You've GOT a gun, right? Ho, ho, ho.

Just a little harmless Wacky Gun Nut humor, there.

But, seriously. All you need is pretty much unlimited time, a fair amount of money, a relentless obsessive pursuit of your goal, and some good networking and intel. Nothing to it!

For more than a year there, ammo was so scarce that all the regular outlets limited customers to 3 boxes of ammo, and in some cases, even a single box. We Ammo Line regulars speculated that soon the poor clerk would auction off single bullets on a little velvet pillow.

Walmart's prices cannot be beat. Find out from the Sporting Goods Department manager what days and time new ammo is put on the shelves. Be very nice to these people. Cookies and homemade Lemon Bars help. The ammo drought is not their fault and they don't appreciate being verbally abused.

Did you know that Walmart has a phone app that will tell you what is in stock? Sadly, my technological skill level is below that of the average 3-year-old. I'm the only woman in America who cannot reliably take photos with my own Verizon Crap Phone, or even answer it without it going all meshuggah on me and whimsically dialing a conference call in Guam. But I have friends who aren't intimidated by an app who will share intel. (See: Cookies and/or Lemon Bars.) Some of these friends will check 4 or 5 different Walmarts in the Phoenix metro area every day. That's where the unlimited time part comes in. And the obsessiveness.

If you learn from the app that 225 round boxes of Remington .22LR Golden Bullets are coming to Casa Grande, and will be put on the shelves at 7:00 a.m., then get there at 6:30 or earlier. (Once, to secure 3 thousand-round boxes of M-22 Winchester ammo, one determined, insomniac buddy and I got there at 2:00 for my first all-nighter since college. It was less fun than I remembered. Not to mention that the ammo does not reliably go "Bang." You might as well throw it at the target.)

Gun shows used to be a good place for bulk ammo, but the last one I attended had .22LR ammo for 35 cents a round, more than you'd pay for 9 millimeter. I pay between five and ten cents a round at Walmart for .22s. So, thanks anyway, but no. Nothing against a fair profit.

But there's such a thing as karma, pal. Just sayin'.

I LOVE MY GUNS

April 26, 2014

Bill Maher, famous One-Percenter donor of one million dollars to Obama's 2012 campaign, wants us to know that despite looking like he would lose a pillowfight with Pajama Boy, he is one macho, strapped-up, packin' dude who has at least one gun. But – unlike those crazy, wacko Republicans – he does not LOVE guns. No, he thinks of them as necessary, you know, "like antibiotics," but has no abiding affection for them.

A man who spends as much time at the Playboy Mansion as Maher is reputed to do would have an understandable fondness for penicillin.

(Bonus joke: How many blondes does it take to change a diaper? Answer: I don't know – ask Hugh Hefner.)

I was under the impression that the only sin in liberalism was being judgmental. So why the snotty bit singling out Republicans as being weirdly enamored of their guns? If there are righteous Democrats among us, speak now and forever hold your piece. Libertarians?

People "love" all kinds of inanimate things. They love cars. To me, a car is just a thing to get me from Point A to Point B with both points involving food. I tend to drive my cars until they die. But I do not disparage the serious Motor Heads among us, from Jay Leno to the brilliant Iowahawk nor suggest that there is anything fundamentally wrong with them.

Women, on the other hand, "love" shoes and handbags (what

we, in both MN and AZ call "purses"). Ammo Grrrll was taking a potty break in the gender line in Heaven when those affinities were passed out. Shoes – along with shirts — are something to wear to meet health code standards in restaurants, except in Hawaii. And purses? I have dear, misguided female friends who own purses that cost hundreds, even thousands of dollars. It pains me to think of the ammo that could buy! If I spend thousands for a purse, it better come with a Kimber Master Carry Custom .45 ACP inside, at a minimum, and maybe an Ed Brown.

Neither do I have fancy fingernails which would interfere with loading a magazine.

A blissfully happy, unbitter clinger, I love my God, my husband, my children, my parents, siblings, and dozens of wonderful friends. And I also love my Sig Sauer P229 Black Elite 9 millimeter handgun. A sweet, beautiful, and deadly-accurate weapon. I love my little Ruger SR22, the first handgun I ever owned. And soon, I will love my next gun: the Walther PPQ, striker-fired, 9 millimeter semi-automatic pistol. The trigger is awesome. Try it, you'll love it!

And Bill? Go jump in a grotto.

CASHIER IN FRY'S

May 2, 2014

You know that scene in *The Wizard of Oz* where Dorothy says, "We aren't in Kansas any more, Toto"?

We had only been back in our dusty little village (DLV) in Arizona for a few weeks after the summer break when we were shopping for groceries at Fry's. My husband picked up *Conceal and Carry* Magazine and added it to the pile. Our checkout lady was an attractive African-American woman who also may or may not have been gay. Wouldn't bet the ranch either way. And couldn't care less.

To our surprise, she picked up the magazine and actually started thumbing through it. Uh-oh, we thought. In Minnesota, as a member of at least 2 and possibly 3 protected groups, she could have summoned Security and claimed that the magazine had made her feel threatened or – my favorite bogus charge – "uncomfortable." ("You have the right to remain comfortable. Anything anyone says or does that makes you uncomfortable can be litigated…as long as you aren't a white Christian male who likes women…")

But, no. We aren't IN Kansas any more, remember?

"What do you carry?" she asks, conversationally. Somewhat flummoxed, my husband answered her.

"I carry a .25," she says, "I want to put 'em DOWN, not just scare 'em." "Are you sure a .25 will put 'em down?" asked my husband. And she replied, "I'm a very good shot!"

Well, OK. Bless your little heart, sister. Now, I don't know where this lady lives. Our DLV has just been rated the 8th safest town in Arizona. But what was most striking at the last gun show I attended was just how many women, elderly people and people with disabilities were shopping for weapons. In other words, the most vulnerable among us – looking for Mr. Colt's "equalizer" or at least a sporting chance.

When we women were younger, we could convince ourselves that we could possibly fight our way out of trouble. We were undoubtedly grievously mistaken. Testosterone is just a terribly unfair advantage! But, once we hit 60, say, no matter how many Zumba classes we have attended, it becomes crystal clear that we are sitting ducks. And, make no mistake, thugs go for the easiest targets. Counting on a thug to say, "Oh, Jeez, I didn't see your wheelchair, there, never mind," is a pipe-dream. Ladies, forget your traditional friends, Ben and Jerry. Count on Mr. Smith, Mr. Wesson or their Austrian cousin, the super-reliable Mr. Glock.

MATH IS HARD!

September 5, 2014

Remember, in one of the incarnations of the Barbie Doll she was programmed to say, "Math is hard!"? And whoa! What a fuss that caused in the Perpetually Furious Grievance Quarters! (Bonus favorite t-shirt slogan: "You think it's offensive, I think it's funny; that's why I'm a much happier person than you are.")

Imagine the effect on a little girl hearing a doll say that! Why, then, all the little girls who take life-coaching advice from inanimate objects would be forced to assume that Math is hard. And rather than concluding that she would just have to work and study to succeed, the little girl would have no choice but to abandon her dream of a career in astrophysics to become a stripper. Assuming the poor little ninny can count bills in various denominations. ("Oh, fudge, I was told there would be no math involved in stripping! Cuz Math is hard!")

So, how much ammo separates the target-shooting enthusiast from the dangerous nutjob? Let's say that a neighbor of one Mr. John Johnson doesn't like the cut of his jib and calls the cops to report that she thinks he has way too many guns and too much ammo in his house.

Frequently when the homes of suspected Wacko Gun Nuts are invaded, reporters put on the Look of Grave Concern they learned in Broadcast School and tell us in breathless tones that "John Wayne Harvey Bubba Johnson, suspected Tea Party member, had over TWO HUNDRED ROUNDS of live ammunition!" (which for non-shooters' info, would be two boxes about the size of a couple Altoid tins stacked atop one another. In a word, nothing.)

They always specify that the ammunition is "live" which sounds scary, as if the bullets have a life of their own like Chucky. Invariably, Mr. Johnson turns out to be a drab, disappointing registered Democrat. His scary stash consists of his childhood .22 rifle and one legal handgun in a lockbox. Unfortunately, his door was breached with a battering ram and though Mr. Johnson was not home, SWAT fired 1,458 rounds at his cat, several of which hit it, using up all 9 of its lives.

Since Mr. Johnson did not turn out to be the elusive terrorist Tea Party member who would make Chris Mathews' leg tingle into a source of clean energy, we never hear from Mr. Johnson again unless and until his wrongful death suit on behalf of the cat wends its way through the courts. Regretting that it was Mr. Snuggles and not Mr. Johnson who was killed, PETA files an amicus brief.

Math is hard. And 200 rounds are, I repeat, nothing, although felonious in some states. A target shooter can run through that in a pleasant half-hour at the range and that includes loading your magazines by hand. Multiply that times a summer of even once-weekly shooting, and you see the math of it. Like a certain avid golfer, it is not unusual for me to enjoy my sport three times a week, although I seldom babble blandly about beheadings before hustling to the range. Which is why standing in an ammo line is a part-time job. And one I'm very good at. If you need anything at the Post Office or the DMV, I'm your craven ravin' hillbilly grrrll.

WALMART AMMO SALE

October 17, 2014

Any shooter who hasn't been in a medically-induced coma for the last two years knows that .22 ammo has been scarcer than functional hard-drives at the IRS. Given the title of my Friday guest column and my "handle," you can guess that I am known around my Dusty Little Village (DLV) in Arizona for being keenly interested in accumulating ammo.

When it is hot in Arizona (March through November), I frequently do my daily walk at Walmart. There are multiple bathrooms, a climate controlled environment, water fountains, no mosquitoes, and doughnuts as a reward for walking for an hour. Or so. No need to keep obsessive track of the time. Do you think it is a sign of the Apocalypse or simply a sign that a person has no life if she knows the names of 42 individual Walmart employees?

On the last day of September, one of the managers (Tattoo Mike as opposed to Kneepad Mike, recovering from knee surgery) excitedly informed me that Walmart had been stockpiling cases and cases of .22 ammo and was fixin' to have a huge sale! Color me happy! Not just any crappy old .22s either, but CCIs, the Cadillac of .22 ammo.

"OMG," I said, in all caps. "When?"

And he said, "This coming Saturday."

"OMG," I repeated in sorrow and disbelief. "Saturday is Yom Kippur, the holiest day of the Jewish year! I can't eat, drink, spend money or drive. And we spend all day praying."

Tattoo Mike had never heard of Yom Kippur. So much for multiculturalism. Now, I don't mind at all when gentiles, even store personnel, wish me a "Merry Christmas." I say it right back. I was amused, not offended when the cashier at Byerly's supermarket in St. Paul put a "Sale on Easter Ham" leaflet into my grocery bag, despite its being filled with Kosher for Passover food. I did not call a whiny press conference when the clueless little girl at the same market's post office counter gave me stamps with the Baby Jesus on them for what I specifically told her were my Hanukkah cards.

But a Yom Kippur ammo sale? That I could not even attend!? That is something up with which I could not put.

I begged Tattoo Mike to sell me some the day before. He said management had anticipated possible shenanigans and the cash registers wouldn't even allow it. I hinted broadly at a religious discrimination suit and casually mentioned that Mr. Ammo Grrrll is, among many many things, an attorney. No dice. I started making a "No justice, no peace" banner. Briefly considered looting or interrupting a symphony. Rejected idea as I do not look good in orange and jumpsuits are not handy for women of late, late middle age who have excitable bladders.

Do you think my neighbor, the Paranoid Texan, or my shooting instructor, or my poker buddy, the Iraqi vet, who stood in line would share their stash with me? Well, heck no. They are all shooters too and Walmart had a limit of 3 boxes to a customer. Each of these men would probably give me a kidney if I needed one. But asking for .22s is over the line. Like ladies in the '50s with their precious books of Green Stamps, some things are just not negotiable. Yom Kippur ended around 7:30 p.m. They had run out of .22s by 1:30.

I'm hoping the next .22 sale is on Christmas Eve to give me a sporting chance. It seems only fair, like when an umpire flubs a call and then later favors the other team in a "make-up" call. But I'm not holding my breath.

LEO ENCOUNTERS

December 5, 2014

If you have never been pulled over by a Law Enforcement Officer of any kind, you are either Lady Luck's own child or very very law-abiding. And good for you either way!

I was pulled over once in Wisconsin in a 1980 VW Rabbit doing 85 in a 55 zone and the guy let me go with a warning because he didn't believe a Rabbit could actually DO 85. Now, admittedly, I was a much younger and marginally-cuter person of the female persuasion and I think we probably have an easier time of it with Highway Patrolmen. But you best believe that I was all about, "Yessir, and no sir, and here's my license and registration, Officer. Sir."

It is one of the first things we told our son when he learned to drive, right after "Always use your seat belts.": Do not be a hostile smart-ass in any encounter with law enforcement officers. Which would not be intuitive for someone with smart-ass genes rolling like a mighty river down both sides of his gene pool. (Or as Mother says, "Plant corn; get corn.")

Several years ago, coming across Texas on the way to California, I saw the dreaded flashing lights behind me and pulled over. An African-American Highway Patrolman asked for license and registration and asserted that I had changed lanes without signaling. Though it is my practice always to signal, it is possible that I did not, since no one had been behind me roughly since Oklahoma. Every Texas driver passed me like I was parked. This Patrolman was not courteous. Now if you say that to anyone in the Grievance Industry they will say that I didn't like him because he was "uppity". No. I didn't like him very much because he was rude. But, seeing my out-of-state plates, he did give me a warning on a little slip of paper touting the "Drive the Texas Friendly Way", for which I thanked him profusely.

For those who see everything through the race prism, I could make a case that this black officer enjoyed the power he had to harass white drivers, that I was a victim of Driving While White. Or I could say that it was a slow, boring day and he just felt like it and race didn't enter into it. He could easily have been an equal opportunity jerk. Or just having a bad day.

A more recent example of a law enforcement officer encounter occurred right here in our Dusty Little Village. A few weeks after Michael Brown made a series of stupid and, ultimately, fatal decisions, The Paranoid Texan Next Door made a right turn onto our main drag. He saw the flashing lights behind him and pulled over immediately. He rarely wears a wife-beater undershirt, so he did not take off in a high speed chase hoping to be featured on an episode of Cops. He did not leave his vehicle to attack the cop.

However, since this is Arizona, what this particular polite, professional, local black cop said even before "License and registration, please," was "Sir, are you carrying a gun?" To which The Paranoid Texan replied, "Yes, sir, I am; it is in an appendix holster on my right. I'm putting my hands on the steering wheel while you remove it."

Which the cop did. He removed the magazine and checked for a round in the chamber.

(When I asked The PT later if he had also given the cop the weapon in the glovebox, he said "No, he never asked about that one." All info from The Paranoid Texan is on a need to know basis. And hence, his name.)

Our friend inquired as to his offense, and the cop said that he had "rolled" through the stop sign without coming to a full and complete stop. Now, the Paranoid Texan is known to all and sundry as someone who speaks Sarcasm as a Second Language. Did he say, "Hey, that's just the way I roll, Law-dawg." No, he did not. He is a wit, not a half-wit.

Once again, just a warning was issued, the officer gave him back his gun and The Paranoid Texan and his life rolled on, though not through any stop signs in the immediate area.

Rich Lowry was bang on when he shocked the liberal mush-minds on Meet the Democrat Press by asserting that the main lesson of Ferguson was (paraphrasing): "don't walk down the middle of the street after committing theft and assault and don't charge a police officer and try to get his gun." Had Michael Brown followed these sane, simple rules, he would be alive today no matter his color or the color of the cop, and nobody would have heard of Ferguson. Several local businesses would still exist.

So, to review:

Wrong way: Charge the officer; punch the officer; grab the officer's gun in his vehicle and say, "You won't shoot me because you're a p***y."

Right way: "Yes, Officer, I agree that I should not be walking down the middle of the street. I am moving to the sidewalk right now, Sir. Would you care for a cigar?"

THINKING ABOUT PLINKING

January 9, 2015

It is 7:00 on a Wednesday morning and just turning from dark to light. It is a beautiful 55 degrees. And I am loading magazines preparatory to going plinking. I got an Israeli-made autoloader for my birthday. Last year I got a gun-cleaning workbench. I'm easy to buy for.

Indoor ranges are fine, but for the most fun you can have with your clothes on, you have to plink in the desert of a beautiful clear morning. The mountains surround you on three sides. The bees are humming in perfect unison at a decibel level that you wouldn't notice with city noises. The sun is just peeking over the horizon and the temperature will eventually drive you back to your air-conditioning or heat, depending on the season. But for now, all is perfect.

Here in the desert, in gay profusion all around us, the evidence exists of the inventive things that others have shot at: old 33 rpm record albums and their covers; retired Hallowe'en pumpkins; bowling pins; watermelons; metal targets that spin when you hit one of the movable arms; hay bales with shredded bullseye targets still on them. Shooters are a convivial lot – they will leave cool stuff to play with. They pick up their brass, though.

I tried shooting at the album covers, but found it too creepy. I'm not comfortable shooting at a picture of Barry Manilow, no matter how much he may have it coming for "I Write the Songs." It felt a lot more personal than shooting at the grey or pink silhouette guys with the concentric circle innards. Or the evil yellow triangles, rogue red circles, and menacing blue squares.

Despite working out with weights three times a week, after two or three hours and several hundred rounds, I readily admit that my hands and arms get tired and I start doing figure-eights. Then I know it's time to go home.

This used to make me feel inadequate until I reasoned that if this small woman of late, late middle age has occasion to be in a gun battle that lasts over two hours, it's probably not going to end at all well. I think the gunfight at our OK Corral lasted a couple of minutes as did the SWAT attack on the Lone Wolf Probably-a-Unitarian Terrorist (Nothing to do with Islam) in Sydney. Not to mention that I'm going to need an assistant to load magazines. And a snack and potty break.("Excuse me, there, zombie bad guys, I had a lot of coffee this morning, so 'talk amongst yourselves'. I'll be back in a minute…and no peeking!")

Just like when I shot with John Hinderaker, my shooting buddies share guns. It gives you a chance to try out a gun before you buy one. People develop loyalties as fanatical as religious loyalties. You've got your Glock devotees, and your Glock haters. I'm a Sig girl myself, though I am also very fond of my Walther PPQ 9 mm. No matter how cool the brand, the gun has to feel right in your hand. And not be a terrible pain in the patootie to field-strip and clean.

When we first moved to Arizona, we attended a fund-raiser for Sheriff Paul Babeu. Later he was outed as gay and nobody in Arizona much cared. Except that he's very good-looking and a friend had him picked out for her niece. Oh, well. Anyhow, they were raffling off an AR-15 at Sheriff Paul's fund-raiser, but ticket sales were really slow. When I asked somebody at our table why, he said, "Because everybody here already has one." Point taken. I love Arizona.

INTERMEZZO: FAVORITES

We all play favorites. Hopefully, not with children, but with colors, friends, foods, clothes, tourist spots. And so it is with artists and writers. Astonishingly-prolific writers like Elmore Leonard or Donald E. Westlake still have their favorite creative works that they mention in interviews.

Power Line is written at such a consistently high level that I am inspired to try to measure up.

I try never to "phone it in", but to work hard on each and every column. Sometimes, I work on a column for several days or even weeks, and tinker with it endlessly. Often, the finished product bears little or no resemblance to the original. Sometimes, I have tinkered all the "funny" out of it.

Other times, it does seem as though an "invisible hand" or "typist" is doing the writing, that the words just flow from my brain and heart to the paper or screen. Sadly, that is not as often as one might wish.

Often I am surprised that a column that I think is pretty darn funny gets very little response and other times, a column that seems kind of "meh" to me really hits the audience's funny bone. It was like that with standup too. When I loved a piece of material, I would give it three or four tries, but if it never hit the mark, I would discard it, no matter how much I liked it.

These five selections are my personal favorites from the first year. I hope you enjoy reading them again.

IN PRAISE OF MEN

July 4, 2014

It was probably about 20 years ago that I first heard the repulsive charge that America has a "rape culture." It has now metastasized into the mainstream, but was a new theme back then. I was hired to entertain at a luncheon for women and girls and the group before me was making a presentation on the subject. Mercifully, I missed most of it, but what I did hear enraged me so badly it took all the strength I had to try to be funny following it.

My first thought was, "You are slandering my beautiful husband, my wonderful brother, my kind and gentle son, my countless decent, responsible male friends. In short, virtually every man I know, not one of whom is a rapist." Not to mention my beloved country.

And, you are full of crap. Dangerously wrong-headed crap. The 50-year assault on all things male, the neutering of America has not been without dire consequences.

So, let's review, ladies of the Perpetually Furious Grievance Crowd:

Do you have all your lady bits intact, particularly the one that triggers sexual pleasure? Then thank God you live in America and kindly shut up. Just for a minute, because you are, in addition to being wrong, terminally boring.

Are you able to leave your home without a male chaperone? Then thank God you live in America and refrain from making scurrilous charges.

Are you able to drive a car? Then thank God you live in America and paint, please, with a slightly less broad brush.

Are you covered in black from head to toe so that the sun never shines on your face?
No? Then thank God you live in America and help publicize the actual War on Women.

If you ARE covered in black from head to toe so that the sun never shines on your face, are you able to practice your religion in peace in this freedom-loving country? Good for you. Maybe you could do something about extending freedom of religion to people living in the countries you came from instead of hoping to restrict our freedom. Just sayin'.

Have you been able to go to school from kindergarten on, and even gone on to college and medical school and law school without having to worry about being kidnapped or having acid thrown in your faces? Then...well, you know the drill.

American men are, in the main, hard-working, chivalrous, brave, protective, and reliable. And have also mastered deodorant, unlike the men of some continents I could mention. They also have strong egalitarian instincts and will respect women who do not whine and who can do their jobs without asking for special privileges.

Just six days after 9/11, one of the first days that planes flew again, I had to go to Montana for a job. We easily forget how traumatized we all were in those days. The plane was small and filled with hunters returning to Billings. I was the only woman on the plane. Did I fear that I would be assaulted, what with the "rape culture" and all? I mean, how vulnerable was THAT? No.

I was never more happy to see a group of large muscular men in my life. A group that was just BEGGING to have someone pull a boxcutter as the last event of his miserable life. I felt protected and they also helped me wrestle my suitcase from the overhead compartment, the dreadful chauvinists. I'm just now recovering from the post-traumatic stress.

A few years before, my husband and I wintered in San Diego. A comedian friend of mine from Virginia came to visit and we took him to a fine seaside restaurant. During the course of dinner, an unmarried tourist couple was involved in a loud drunken argument in which the man turned obscene and abusive. It went on and on escalating in tone. You could cut the tension in the restaurant with a knife as VIRTUALLY EVERY OTHER MAN in the crowded restaurant – gay and straight! – was on the edge of his seat ready to throttle the guy if things turned physical.

I remember once in San Francisco in the 70s, my husband and I were sound asleep when we heard a woman scream. Without even thinking, without a firearm, my young husband ran out to see what was going on. (Nothing, it turned out, thank God.) Males, certainly American males, just seem hard-wired to protect women and children.

In the Colorado theater shooting rampage at least three young men died trying to protect the women they were with. Oh, gotcha, you say – "the shooter was a MAN. And what about real rape and domestic abuse? Sure, women are safe unless it's the men in their lives that are doing the attacking." Yes, that's also true.

Are there evil men, psychotic men, sexually-deviant men in America? Of course there are, just as there are evil and psychotic men in communist China and socialist Norway, and just as there are also evil and psychotic women who drown their children in bathtubs or drive them into lakes or pimp them out to get drugs.

This country has many cultural problems. But promoting or condoning rape is not one of them. So, on this Fourth of July, let me thank American men for protecting us at home and abroad as cops and soldiers, doctors and nurses; for working hard whatever your job and being good husbands and fathers. Women do those things as well, of course. But – just for today – this is not about you.

STOP APOLOGIZING!

November 24, 2014

You may remember when The Lightbringer first got coronated, that he went on a world-wide Apology Tour, apologizing for any crime, real or imagined, that the Unexceptional Country he was elected to represent had committed. Can you name one country with which we have better, healthier relations now than before Obama took it upon himself to apologize on our behalf? This is a lesson learned in every gradeschool playground when confronted with bullies: Groveling never works. It only inflames and encourages them.

Fast forward to the other day when The Great Shirt Scare drove Ebola off the front pages. A genius scientist with the European Space Agency's Rosetta Project achieved an almost impossible feat (after 10 years!) of landing a space probe on comet 67P. And at the jubilant presser he wore a shirt designed for him – by a close woman friend no less — which featured some cartoon cuties in something other than a burqa. And a few jealous, perpetually-enraged feminists, who couldn't land a minnow using dynamite, lost what passes for their minds.

Then came the traditional groveling, tearful apology from the humiliated scientist, very possibly with his job hanging in the balance. He'll probably be fired anyway; like the abrupt resignation of Larry Summers following Harvard faculty's "no-confidence" vote. Let me repeat that groveling never works, never satisfies the slavering lynch mob.

So you may as well die on your feet as live on your knees. Here is what the young scientist should have said instead. You will recognize the third paragraph homage to The Awesome Bard because some battle cries can't be improved upon:

I will wear this shirt every day until it falls off me in tatters. You will be able to smell me coming in time to flee in terror. If you feel 'unsafe' – a popular feminist weasel word – in the presence of cloth cartoon women, let me assure you that you are completely safe. They aren't real and can't hurt you, though they may invite invidious comparisons. You are much safer than the body politic that caves time and again to intolerant loudmouths like you.

Upon this silly harmless shirt, we shall make our stand. When my envious critic accomplishes what I have accomplished, then she can wear a prom dress with her bra on the outside, or a plaid flannel shirt and sweatpants, and I won't say a mumblin' word. Until that time, she can shut her piehole. Now and forever I will wear whatever I damn please."

This story shall the good man teach his son.
From this day to the ending of the world
We few, we happy few, we band of brothers
Shall wear this shirt. Or any others.
And Pajama Boys on Mommy's insurance to age 26
Shall think themselves accurs'd they lack this shirt so full of chicks.
And hold their cocoa and their puny manhoods while any speaks
That fought with us upon St. Crispins Day for science geeks.

Ammo Grrrll plans to order this shirt to wear to Chick-Fil-A on the way back from shooting at pictures of baby seals at the Tactical Range. If there were some other way to offend the sensibilities of these bullies, I would do that, too. Plastic bags? Carbs? A flag pin? An "I Heart Men" button? A rare steak, glass of bourbon and a Lucky Strike? John should run his Miss Universe contest photos every day. Throw in some cheerleaders. Heck, yeah!

I have had it with these tedious, humorless harridans speaking in my name for the last half century. As Obama advised his supporters, we need to "get in their faces," albeit far enough back to avoid the perpetual flying spittle. So, let this be the moment when we begin to heal this sick culture, and we lower the ocean of bullshit. Enough! No more apologies to totalitarian harpies who hate individualism, free speech, differences of opinion and half the human race.

JUST PLAIN FOLKS

January 16, 2015

The President is fond of invoking "The Folks" in his droning speeches. Now, in rural Minnesota, your "folks" are your parents. But he is referring to those "little" people who make up the once-vast middle class in America. The not-rich and unfamous. The God-fearing, gun-totin' clingers. In other words, people he has never ever hung out with in his entire pampered life and has total contempt for; he doesn't have a clue what makes us tick.

And that's cool. I don't pretend to know what it's like to be so rich that I lose track of how many homes I own. Or to be able to spoil someone's wedding reception in order to golf. Or to whine about being flat broke while giving six-figure speeches. Now, praise God, I've never been a homeless junkie either, but I'll tell you what flat broke was for the working poor, Missy Hillary.

In 1976 for example, flat broke was supporting a family of 3 on $3.50 an hour, and driving a battered 1968 Mercury. It was leaving a movie on a rare Date Night and finding your car battery stolen when it's 30 below zero out. The $50 replacement battery was a serious budget-busting crisis. As icing on the cake, the movie was terrible.

So there's rich and there's poor and I did not then and do not now resent the rich. I'm doing much better myself now, thanks for asking. That's what work, education, and a long-term marriage will do for you. The problem arises when Obama or anyone else tries to "pass." Try to pretend you are just plain folks, and you could wind up complaining about the high price of arugula, a burning concern for every Walmart grocery shopper. It sounds like a disease. "My doctor thinks this rash might be arugula, but I'm hoping it's just leprosy."

I was once hired to entertain at a ladies' luncheon in an upscale country club. During lunch, I recounted an embarrassing incident that had happened to me the day before. I had parked in downtown Minneapolis in one of those confusing multi-level parking ramps. When I went to retrieve my Rabbit, it was not where I thought it should be. Oh, God, was it stolen? The ramp personnel were used to this. One of them took me around in his vehicle until we located the car exactly where it had been left. I could have kissed him, but settled for a $5.00 tip.

We all had a nice laugh of recognition about this at the luncheon. A sweet little gazillionaire whose family owns an important Minnesota company piped up, "Oh, yes! I can relate. The last time we were in Paris, we couldn't remember whether we had left the plane at Orly or DeGaulle." Even in this milieu, there was an awkward silence followed by polite laughter. Lost 7-year old sub-compact car in a freezing slush-filled parking ramp; lost private plane in Paris: Not exactly the same, dear, but thanks for playing!

Perhaps the most embarrassing moment of Obama's many off-teleprompter gaffes, for me, was when he was in the Nationals booth after chucking out the first pitch of the 2010 season's home opener against the White Sox. To say that he threw like a girl is an insult to girls everywhere, including the blind drunk. Sporting a White Sox cap, the President pretended to be a long-time fan, even though he had previously called their ballpark Cominskey rather than Comiskey. The guys in the booth were thrilled to have him there and took him at his word that he had undying devotion to the White Sox. I mean, he had lived in Chicago for years. Color man, Rob Dibble, opened with a question.

Did he ask him to explain the infield fly rule, or to weigh in on the relative merits of the Designated Hitter? No, he did not. The first Nerf toss was to ask who had been his favorite Sox players. He could not name a single White Sox player, current, past or old-timey. Not one. He clearly didn't know the White Sox from the Red Sox from tube socks. Would you not think that his handlers would have at least written down a couple of players for him to mention? Frank Thomas or Luis Aparicio, say.

There is no shame in not knowing baseball, especially for a guy who spent his youth in a madrassa in Indonesia. Fine. All I know about hockey, for example, is that the players are on skates; if they beat an opponent senseless, they get a brief "time-out" in The Box of the Penalty (longer for stabbing or shooting); and, for some reason, they compete for a Big Gulp cup owned by a guy named Stan. Also, Gordie Howe and Bobby Orr are frequent crossword answers. In short, I'm a hockey ignoramus (ignorama?), but I do not lie about being a rabid hockey fan.

Anyway, after doing his patented rambling stammer, Obama allowed as how he liked the Cubs, too. He claimed that growing up in Hawaii he had been a fan of the Oakland A's. Dibble did not ask him to name any Cubs or A's, or even see if he could identify Mickey Mantle or Henry Aaron, probably because the Secret Service had a gun aimed at his privates by then.

Pathetic. I can understand lying about something trivial like Benghazi or our health care system, but what kind of sociopath lies about sports?

THINGS I KNOW FOR SURE ABOUT SEX

January 30, 2015

One: If you get caught on a plane called "The Lolita Express" or on a boat called "Monkey Business" (is there a train called "The Appalling Old Degenerate"?), you should have to wear a hat emblazoned with "Somehow My Weenie Ate My Brain!"

Two: In the endless, tedious discussions about "rape culture," over and over I read testimony from coeds – adult women! – who willingly get into bed with guys and then are amazed when sex occurs. Is there some parallel universe where that is considered unusual?

The reason I ask is that I can say with dead certainty that I have never in my entire life gotten nekkid into bed with a male person without the expectation, nay the fervent hope, that sex could occur. But that's just me.

Help me out here, young ladies, because I'm pretty Old School. How humiliating can it be if you get naked with a guy and yet you expect no response? ("Hey, nuthin' to see here. Just your average naked woman from the dorm next door hoping to catch a few Zs while you watch ESPN. Carry on.") Here we have a generation of women who have been putting condoms on cucumbers since kindergarten who apparently do not have even a passing acquaintance with actual male sexuality.

True, after many many decades of marriage, sometimes you both say, "Good Night, Dear" and go to sleep. But with an unclothed man and an unclothed woman in a nice warm bed, well, you can't ever make book on nothing happening. (Insert childish "over/under" betting joke here.) Men might miss subtle hints. But your average healthy man, finding a naked woman in his bed of her own free will, takes that as a big fat clue that he might get lucky.

If you don't want that, what in blue blazes are you doing there?

So, let's say you accuse a man of "rape" and this is your tale of woe: "Well, we were pretty drunk. I got into bed with this naked guy that I had had sex with before. We did a bunch of drugs. We did some stuff that Bill Clinton said wasn't sex anyway, but I was so wasted I think I passed out and I may or may not have missed the finale. This happened two years ago, and I was fine until Spike, my Feminist Studies professor, informed me I had been raped. Now I'm a hero fighting against sexual assault. I've met Joe Biden! Oh, also, I had sex with him (my 'rapist,' not Joe Biden) a few times after that. But he's kinda mad at me now."

You do not want me on that jury. You really don't. Ladies, I find such narratives an embarrassment to my gender and an affront to actual rape victims, several of whom I have known. Oh, trust me, their stories are nothing at all like yours and involve ugly weapons, grave threats to their lives, and grievous bodily harm. Your whiney tales are not embarrassing just because you had crappy sex – we can discuss the soul-deadening misery of the loveless hookup culture at another time — but because you won't take ownership of your part in it. And are now planning to utterly ruin a man's life over, basically, nothing. Which makes you a liar and a coward. At least one of these *causes célèbre* originated after Mommy found the adult daughter's diary and blew a gasket.

Of course in academia there are no actual trials or juries of peers. The right to representation, to face your accuser, even to know the charges against you, is so yesterday. Every day is Kafka Day on campus. These things used to be called "he said;

she said" situations. Now, it's just "she said; and said and said."
With a great big megaphone from the Grievance Industry and a
Title Nine bludgeon from the Federal government. Two young
adults go out for an evening of drinking and hookup sex. One
goes on to fame and fortune as a brave battler against sexual
"assault". One has his life utterly destroyed. Who, then, was the
predator we hear so much about, and who the prey?

If an adult woman consensually participates in sex and the worst
thing that happens is that she manages to fall asleep at some
point, the consequences pale in comparison with the life-altering
disaster of being falsely accused of rape. You don't have to
register for life as a person who slept through sex. Granted, you
might not want that on your Facebook profile. You also don't
have to wonder how you will ever get a job after being kicked out
of college. Assuming you are lucky enough to avoid or survive
prison.

I try to examine my soul about whether I would feel different
about the disgusting "rape culture" falsehoods if I were the
mother of daughters instead of sons. I don't think so. Not only
am I a woman myself, of course, but I'm pretty sure I would
advise an adult daughter (among many things) not to go into
biker bars in Daisy Dukes and tube tops; not to get too drunk to
drive or to keep an eye on her drink at all times; and definitely
not to get into bed with a naked man unless she expects to have
sex. And quite soon.

Just wait until the first woman is accused by another woman of
sexual assault. It's only a matter of time if it hasn't happened
already. Then how will the unhinged "Women never lie" crowd
know whom to exalt as a heroic victim and whom to crucify as a
rapist?

PIVOTING TO JOBS

February 20, 2015

Every few months, this wretched Administration announces with great fanfare that, having succeeded in ruining everything else, it is now going to "pivot" to jobs. Of course, as anyone who has ever played basketball knows, you pivot enough, you just go in circles, unless your pivot foot slips and you get called for the ancient foul of "traveling." Now in the NBA you can walk the ball from the door of your mansion to the basket, no problem. But I digress.

The pivot happened again last week, only they weren't even pretending to talk about American workers. No, we need to provide jobs for psychotic jackasses lest they become jihadis. Michelle Malkin had her usual brilliant takedown on the "poverty" of the leading jihadis. Well worth a read – take notes! – if you missed it.

But this strategy is surely worth a try. Why, I remember when Granddad, fresh from a stint in the Crusades, sat me on his knee and said, "Honey, we are so bleeping marginalized. We are one of the few families in this little South Dakota town that is neither Norwegian nor even Lutheran. I have no job except trying to raise a few pigs in the back yard. If I don't get a job pretty soon, I may be forced to behead someone. It's one of the few perks of marginalization."

And Grandma just nodded and continued cooking for her tiny cafe where you could get (true story) roast beef, mashed potatoes, a slice of homemade bread and butter and a piece of apple pie for a quarter. She had a job that she created herself but it only occupied her about 15 hours a day so she had plenty of time to sew orange jumpsuits for the doomed.

Down the block (another true story) there lived a man whose enterprising 10-year-old son had a popcorn wagon and this kid made more money in a week (sometimes several dollars) than the man himself did. So, the man had no choice, no choice at all, but to go to the neighboring town and kidnap all the female persons and "marry" them off to his friends. Who could blame him, being underemployed and all? On the way back, he dropped in to the high school to behead the teacher in front of the students. Yay – job opening!

Yes, during the Depression, what with 25 percent of the workforce unemployed, and the other 75 percent mostly underemployed, there was a lot of beheading, crucifixion, kidnapping, stoning, and immolation. These side effects of unemployment have been hitherto relatively unknown but that will be corrected with Depression History Month coming up in August right after High Horse Month where all the terrible, no good, very bad things that Christians and Jooz have done will be highlighted. (Sure, you might think the Salk polio vaccine and Wasserman tests for syphilis were good, but, hey, autism!)

Meanwhile, back in South Dakota, because of unemployment, all the young girls also had to have mutilation of important lady bits, and several "bachelor" farmers were thrown off the barns and stoned if they survived. What a lot of bad stuff can happen when you don't have a good job! After the Depression, that little popcorn wagon boy became a multimillionaire (still true story) and prosperity reigned. Beheadings tapered off to almost nothing.

A SPECIAL BONUS

Jay Comeau was a very special commenter. Though Scott and the boys tried hard to enforce some kind of standards for commenters – no naughty words, no personal attacks – to keep discussion on a higher plane than most of the Internet, Jay would go right up to that line and put a toe across. Sometimes a whole foot and part of a leg.

Jay was a big fan of my column and a regular commenter on all the Power Line articles. He reached out to Power Line and asked them to forward an email on to me. We became penpals. Jay used to email me his writings. He asked for my comments and criticism. He wanted more than almost anything to be a bona fide writer. He clearly had talent and I encouraged him.

He was almost hilariously un-self-confident. If I took over 3 minutes to respond to an emailed piece of material, he just knew that it meant that I had hated it. "Uh, no, Jay, it means that I was at the grocery store or not up yet. Remember, in Florida, you are 3 HOURS ahead of me in time! We don't do Daylight Savings Time!" He also refused to get a computer with Word on it. I thought I was truly the bottom of the barrel for technologically baffled, but I am Bill Freakin' Gates next to him. He sent me all his writing using only email, despite my explaining to him multiple times that one cannot submit an article or novel via email.

Jay worked up this piece about his trip to what was then East Germany when he was a "kid". I really liked it and I asked my editor, Scott, if he would print it in lieu of my column one week. He declined, which was totally his right. As an attorney, I think he placed a great deal of emphasis on "precedent" and he did not want me to just invite friends and relatives willy-nilly to sub in for me. I was quite enough of a loose cannon. The Power Line boys have worked hard to have a terrific "brand", and they protect that brand very fiercely. And more power to them.

I am extremely fond of this piece. I did help Jay punch it up a bit. I was about to beg Scott once again to give it a chance, when Jay passed away suddenly on June 2, 2017. I don't know if I have ever been more affected by the loss of a person not related to me. So, Jay, buddy, wherever you are currently causing trouble, and going right up to the line in your double entendres, here you are in print. We miss you more than words can say.

JAY COMEAU
"Welcome to Workers' Paradise"

In 1984, my then-fiance and I were backpacking around Europe and Morocco. When the occasion arose to mention an occupation, I would put down "freelance writer." With an emphasis on the "free" part. And who among us is not? While in Amsterdam – it makes me blush to think of it – I told my fiance that I thought we needed some "space". She put up a disappointingly-small fuss upon hearing this tragic news.

My stated intention was to go to Berlin for a week. My Europass only got me to the border of East Germany, so I decided to hitchhike. My German was limited to "Guten Tag", which starts the day off right, and then the ability to count to three. Perhaps I would find someone who liked to waltz.

A young lady who I had given directions earlier in enthusiastic sign language, picked me up. She was a very skittish girl and made me sit in the back seat. We crossed into East Germany on the only road into or out of Berlin that connected West and East. No exits allowed. No service plazas. An above-ground Holland tunnel.

The language barrier was hilarious. She would speak; I would speak; and neither of us had a clue what had been said. It was like a bad marriage without the rancor. Although she did

150

eventually let me into the front seat, alas, we parted ways soon after we made it into West Berlin. It was just after dark. I found a cheap room, a cheaper bar and made plans to make it into East Berlin the next morning.

I failed to find the notorious "Checkpoint Charlie", so I made my way to Freidrichstrasse. After exchanging hard western currency for the near-worthless East German marks, I got the coveted exotic stamp in my passport: Jay Comeau, Man of Mystery, Fearless Traveler!

Once inside, the first thing I noticed was how drab everything was. The vibrancy of West Berlin was in stark contrast to the utter grayness surrounding me. Who doesn't love guard shacks on every block? And everywhere, the propaganda posters showing happy revelers in Nicaragua and Cuba.

But young people are young people and the beer halls were pretty cheery. I spent my marks as freely as I could on brats and beer so cheap it would normally have made me weep with joy. But, I was on a DAY PASS and was told the penalty was harsh for overstaying. Even harsher than our own visa overstays today. Haha. I kid.

I spotted what for East Berlin was virtually a luxury hotel and went to the lounge to dribble away the rest of my marks. My brave excursion into communism was winding down.

Wrong! Some Russian athletes were at the bar and when they found I was an Americanski, the shots just kept on flowing. There are some parts that are a little fuzzy after that, but when I sobered up, it was two days later and I was still in East Berlin on an expired day pass. Uh-oh.

My paper day pass struck me as evidence against me, so decided to lose that. One had to exit where one entered, so I made my way back to Freidrichstrasse. I hit on the cunning plan of going at 5 p.m., hoping the rush hour traffic would provide a bit of cover. It didn't.

The authorities were not even a little amused when I could not produce my day pass. I was sent to a senior official's office and told to wait outside as his Charge D'Affaires catalogued my misdeeds. As I sat there, contemplating life in a gulag, I noticed a small silk banner featuring crossed flags of East Germany and the Soviet Union with the proclamation: "Deutch/Sowiet Freundsschaft" or as close as I remember.

In for a penny, in for a pound. I did what any 26-year-old idiot, raised in the ever-forgiving confines of the U.S.A would do – I swiped it. Right off the glass wall of the guy who was going to determine my fate.

Eventually the superior came out, lectured me severely about my irresponsibility and allowed me to exit East Berlin. Nobody could take ownership of irresponsibility like me in those days. I have always wondered when they noticed the silk banner was gone. But I was safe in West Berlin, still surrounded by East Germany, still on thin ice.

My transit visa expired, I now faced getting out of West Berlin and back to the safety of West Germany. Buoyed by my East Berlin escapade, I rejected the idea of crawling to the authorities for a new transit visa. I was now beyond that. I was James Bond's slow brother, Jay Bond, born to nick office decorations, licensed to kill time.

I managed to hitch my way out to a truck stop on the border of the Allied Zone. In the cafe I overheard a driver say the word "Cologne". I asked for a ride. He asked if I had papers. "Yes," I lied. By now, such lies were child's play. He spoke very limited English but we connected through the International language of music, rolling through the night to Steely Dan.

Eventually, I had to admit that I had no papers. He stuffed me in the sleeping part of his truck, buried me in bedding and told me to remain absolutely silent, not one of the aces in my skill set. We rolled through the frontier checkpoint and I was once again free from totalitarianism.

It was years later that I told my parents about this escapade. The only part that disappointed my Dad was that, somehow, my little silk banner had gotten away from me. I would give almost anything I own to have it back.

AFTERWORD

Well, there you have it, friends. The first year of columns all gathered in one handy dandy place. I left out only a couple columns that, in retrospect, I felt weren't as strong or as humorous. As my late, great Mama would say, they were "not up to snuff". I have no idea how a gross tobacco product figures in to excellence, but, that's the expression. If I didn't like them all that much, I saw no reason to inflict them on readers a second time.

Hey, if a baseball player is considered a wild success for making contact with the ball one out of three times, I figure 2 or 3 "meh" columns out of 52 is a pretty good batting average.

So, you now own Volume I of what will eventually be a good-sized collection of columns. Thank you. I would encourage you to check in to Power Line several times a day at www.powerlineblog.com, and for sure on Fridays when my new weekly column appears.

While you are at it, I have another splendid opportunity for you to be entertained. You could buy my husband's wonderful first novel: *Khaybar, Minnesota* by (his nom de plume) Max Cossack. We both will thank you for it, especially if you review it on Amazon with no fewer than FIVE stars! Please.

If you DID like either book, please tell your friends, or buy a whole bunch of the books and mail them out at the reasonable and cheap "Book Rate" at your U.S. Post Office. Such a deal!

And if you did NOT like the book, please, feel free to tell the people you heartily dislike about the books and encourage them to fritter away their hard-earned money on them. Thank you.

If you would like your paperback version personally autographed, please send a check made out to VWAM for $2.00 (per book) to:

VWAM (Ammo Grrrll)
P.O. Box 618
Maricopa, AZ 85139

Include the name you wish me to sign it to, and any BRIEF thing in particular you would like me to say. Otherwise, it will just say "Best Wishes" with my signature.

Example: "To Nancy, from Grandpa" Merry Christmas!
Or, "To Cletus, from Uncle George" Welcome home from prison!

Or, if for yourself and not a gift: "To Daniel" We'll always have Paris!

I will write pretty much anything that's not obscene.

If you would like me to fire a .22 round into the peel-and-stick label before autographing it, please include a third dollar.
Thank you and God Bless Us Every One!

Love from Susan Vass (Ammo Grrrll)
Maricopa, Arizona, November of 2018

Cover by coversbykaren.com
(an excellent artist and patient woman)